DATA SECURITY: EXAMINING EFFORTS TO PROTECT AMERICANS' FINANCIAL INFORMATION

HEARING

BEFORE THE

SUBCOMMITTEE ON FINANCIAL INSTITUTIONS AND CONSUMER CREDIT

OF THE

COMMITTEE ON FINANCIAL SERVICES

U.S. HOUSE OF REPRESENTATIVES

ONE HUNDRED THIRTEENTH CONGRESS

SECOND SESSION

MARCH 5, 2014

Printed for the use of the Committee on Financial Services

Serial No. 113–68

U.S. GOVERNMENT PRINTING OFFICE

88–530 PDF WASHINGTON : 2014

For sale by the Superintendent of Documents, U.S. Government Printing Office
Internet: bookstore.gpo.gov Phone: toll free (866) 512–1800; DC area (202) 512–1800
Fax: (202) 512–2104 Mail: Stop IDCC, Washington, DC 20402–0001

HOUSE COMMITTEE ON FINANCIAL SERVICES

JEB HENSARLING, Texas, *Chairman*

GARY G. MILLER, California, *Vice Chairman*
SPENCER BACHUS, Alabama, *Chairman Emeritus*
PETER T. KING, New York
EDWARD R. ROYCE, California
FRANK D. LUCAS, Oklahoma
SHELLEY MOORE CAPITO, West Virginia
SCOTT GARRETT, New Jersey
RANDY NEUGEBAUER, Texas
PATRICK T. McHENRY, North Carolina
JOHN CAMPBELL, California
MICHELE BACHMANN, Minnesota
KEVIN McCARTHY, California
STEVAN PEARCE, New Mexico
BILL POSEY, Florida
MICHAEL G. FITZPATRICK, Pennsylvania
LYNN A. WESTMORELAND, Georgia
BLAINE LUETKEMEYER, Missouri
BILL HUIZENGA, Michigan
SEAN P. DUFFY, Wisconsin
ROBERT HURT, Virginia
MICHAEL G. GRIMM, New York
STEVE STIVERS, Ohio
STEPHEN LEE FINCHER, Tennessee
MARLIN A. STUTZMAN, Indiana
MICK MULVANEY, South Carolina
RANDY HULTGREN, Illinois
DENNIS A. ROSS, Florida
ROBERT PITTENGER, North Carolina
ANN WAGNER, Missouri
ANDY BARR, Kentucky
TOM COTTON, Arkansas
KEITH J. ROTHFUS, Pennsylvania

MAXINE WATERS, California, *Ranking Member*
CAROLYN B. MALONEY, New York
NYDIA M. VELÁZQUEZ, New York
BRAD SHERMAN, California
GREGORY W. MEEKS, New York
MICHAEL E. CAPUANO, Massachusetts
RUBÉN HINOJOSA, Texas
WM. LACY CLAY, Missouri
CAROLYN McCARTHY, New York
STEPHEN F. LYNCH, Massachusetts
DAVID SCOTT, Georgia
AL GREEN, Texas
EMANUEL CLEAVER, Missouri
GWEN MOORE, Wisconsin
KEITH ELLISON, Minnesota
ED PERLMUTTER, Colorado
JAMES A. HIMES, Connecticut
GARY C. PETERS, Michigan
JOHN C. CARNEY, Jr., Delaware
TERRI A. SEWELL, Alabama
BILL FOSTER, Illinois
DANIEL T. KILDEE, Michigan
PATRICK MURPHY, Florida
JOHN K. DELANEY, Maryland
KYRSTEN SINEMA, Arizona
JOYCE BEATTY, Ohio
DENNY HECK, Washington

SHANNON McGAHN, *Staff Director*
JAMES H. CLINGER, *Chief Counsel*

Subcommittee on Financial Institutions and Consumer Credit

SHELLEY MOORE CAPITO, West Virginia, *Chairman*

SEAN P. DUFFY, Wisconsin, *Vice Chairman*
SPENCER BACHUS, Alabama
GARY G. MILLER, California
PATRICK T. McHENRY, North Carolina
JOHN CAMPBELL, California
KEVIN McCARTHY, California
STEVAN PEARCE, New Mexico
BILL POSEY, Florida
MICHAEL G. FITZPATRICK, Pennsylvania
LYNN A. WESTMORELAND, Georgia
BLAINE LUETKEMEYER, Missouri
MARLIN A. STUTZMAN, Indiana
ROBERT PITTENGER, North Carolina
ANDY BARR, Kentucky
TOM COTTON, Arkansas

GREGORY W. MEEKS, New York, *Ranking Member*
CAROLYN B. MALONEY, New York
RUBEN HINOJOSA, Texas
CAROLYN McCARTHY, New York
DAVID SCOTT, Georgia
AL GREEN, Texas
KEITH ELLISON, Minnesota
NYDIA M. VELÁZQUEZ, New York
STEPHEN F. LYNCH, Massachusetts
MICHAEL E. CAPUANO, Massachusetts
PATRICK MURPHY, Florida
JOHN K. DELANEY, Maryland
DENNY HECK, Washington

CONTENTS

DATA SECURITY: EXAMINING EFFORTS TO PROTECT AMERICANS' FINANCIAL INFORMATION

Wednesday, March 5, 2014

U.S. HOUSE OF REPRESENTATIVES,
SUBCOMMITTEE ON FINANCIAL INSTITUTIONS AND CONSUMER CREDIT,
COMMITTEE ON FINANCIAL SERVICES,
Washington, D.C.

The subcommittee met, pursuant to notice, at 10:03 a.m., in room 2128, Rayburn House Office Building, Hon. Shelley Moore Capito [chairwoman of the subcommittee] presiding.

Members present: Representatives Capito, Bachus, McHenry, Pearce, Posey, Fitzpatrick, Luetkemeyer, Stutzman, Pittenger, Barr, Cotton, Rothfus; Meeks, Maloney, Scott, Green, Lynch, Delaney, and Heck.

Ex officio present: Representatives Hensarling and Waters.

Also present: Representatives Royce and Sinema.

Chairwoman CAPITO. The subcommittee will come to order. Without objection, the Chair is authorized to declare a recess of the subcommittee at any time.

I now recognize myself for the purpose of making an opening statement.

Over the last 6 months, we have learned about a series of breaches of American businesses' data—millions and millions have had their personal data compromised. We will not know the true extent of the impact on American consumers until investigators from Federal agencies and private entities are done with the investigation.

These breaches raise, I believe, really legitimate questions about the storage and usage of personal data by private industry. The prosperous have long sought access to this type of information, but the recent breaches demonstrated an evolving sophistication of attacks that seek to exploit and confuse consumers.

As we have learned in previous subcommittee hearings, these criminals often reside in nations that fail to cooperate with United States law enforcement agencies. In some cases, these nations not only protect these criminals from prosecution but they celebrate them as heros.

The data these criminals steal is often sold on the black market and can potentially be used for fraudulent purposes. While possibilities for such fraudulent charges may be the source of stress and frustration for consumers, many payment networks have zero fraud policies to protect consumers from fraudulent transactions.

Today, we will learn more about why these breaches are occurring, existing payment security standards, what happens during and after a breach, and new payment technologies authorized to help prevent future breaches.

One area that is of critical importance is information-sharing, both during and after a breach.

We have representatives from the National Cybersecurity and Communications Integration Center (NCCIC) and the Financial Services Information Sharing and Analysis Center (FS-ISAC) who will testify about the existing information-sharing efforts between the private sector and government agencies. On February 13th, members of the retail financial services communities publicly announced their efforts at information-sharing amongst all parties that are a part of the payment system. I applaud this effort instructing all parties to strive for a more efficient, thorough, and effective information-sharing system to prevent data breaches in the future.

The final area that this hearing will cover is future payment systems that may provide consumers with a more secure method of transmitting their financial data. I have great interest in the progression and diversification of our payment system. In the past, we learned about developments in mobile payments. Today, we will learn about a cloud-based tokenization proposal which will transfer payments without the need to store significant amounts of consumer financial data.

If sensitive payment data is not being stored unnecessarily, the payment systems could be much less attractive to future hackers. The high degree of innovation in the payment space is exciting for consumers, but we also need to ensure that the new payment systems that are developed increase the level of security and reduce the threat of future breaches.

I would like to thank our witnesses for joining us this morning. Each of you plays a critical role in helping to prevent future data breaches.

I now yield time to the ranking member of the subcommittee, Mr. Meeks, for an opening statement.

Mr. MEEKS. Thank you, Madam Chairwoman.

In recent months, a number of banking and U.S. retailers including Target, Neiman Marcus, and Nike have announced data breaches which stole the payment card account and sensitive personal information of millions of Americans. Although forensic investigations of recent breaches are still ongoing, news reports and announcements by the retailers themselves indicate that these breaches may be the largest breaches ever in the history of our country as of today.

On December 19, 2013, Target announced that 40 million credit and debit accounts had been compromised through its in-store credit card magnetic strips, allowing hackers to access customer names, credit and debit card numbers, and security codes. Less than a month later, on January 10, 2014, Target announced that the breach was significantly larger and that the personal information of 70 million customers was also stolen.

Americans need to have the security that when they shop at a retail store, or when they use their credit or their debit cards, their account and personal information will be protected. We must make sure that happens.

It is further troubling that we see the line fall behind Europe and Canada in terms of technology and security standards. Some reports even indicate that we are behind certain countries in Latin America and Africa, who are using the latest mobile technology for processing payments, as a result of the fact that they started late in adopting such technology, and therefore immediately adopted the latest innovations.

We have to improve our technology to make sure that we are more up-to-date. We need to take our security more seriously in this country. The security breaches at Target were only reminders of existing national security issues, and there are, indeed, a lot of issues which we will seek to clarify in our hearing. How is it that this could happen in the world's most advanced economy and financial market in the world?

What have we learned, and how do we prevent these serious incidents from ever happening again? And what technologies and standards need to be adopted instead so that we can protect Americans and the Nation?

I want to thank all of the witnesses who are here, and I look forward to your participation and to listening to your testimony.

Chairwoman CAPITO. Thank you.

I now recognize Mr. Fitzpatrick for 2 minutes for an opening statement.

Mr. FITZPATRICK. Thank you, Madam Chairwoman, for calling this hearing, and I also thank the witnesses for their time today.

I spend a considerable amount of time at home—as do my colleagues—visiting my discrict, visiting with businesses and financial instutions, and also talking to their customers. Most if not all of these groups, when asked, would identify cybersecurity, identity theft, and national safety as a concern.

My staff and I spent some time looking into this and quickly learned that hackers and thieves are by and large not only attacking financial institutions directly and literally downloading customers' back accounts to either deceive people into giving up their security information or they are stealing outright from some other source. Those sources are many times unsuspecting businesses or financial institutions that are storing or transferring personal information in ways that are quite vulnerable to attack.

That is not to say that the burden of data security lies disproportionately with any one group, but I think these facts speak to the importance of working in a collaborative manner on developing a system that protects personal financial data through the process—from the individual, to the business, to the processor, and then to the bank or credit union.

There is a level of trust necessary for an economy to function in this new virtual era, where cash is becoming a preferred payment method for fewer and fewer people. I look forward to the testimony and hearing what these experts can share with us about how we can protect people from theft and maintain and possibly restore trust in our cybersecurity system.

And I thank the Chair.

Chairwoman CAPITO. Thank you.

I now recognize Mrs. Maloney for 2 minutes for an opening statement.

Mrs. MALONEY. I want to thank you, Madam Chairlady, and Ranking Member Meeks, for holding this incredibly important hearing. I would say that most Americans have had their identity stolen, including myself, and it is very costly to law enforcement, and certainly to our stakeholders, our financial institutions, and individuals.

And I am particularly interested in the second panel, the industry itself, and what they have to say on new technologies. Why can't we just protect the number and have transactions take place?

This is something really, really important: When the data breach occurs, the party who is most exposed when you look at it is the consumer. It is typically the retailer that is in the best position to know about the breach, although it is often the bank who discovers the breach before the retailer because the bank notices a spike in fraudulent transactions and then traces it back to the retailer that was breached.

In my opinion, this makes it all much more reasonable to make the banks and financial institutions liable for all the fraudulent transactions that occur after the breach. This would give the banks and financial institutions an incentive to invest publicly in fraud-detecting technologies, which are remarkably effective at identifying fraudulent activities on your credit or debit card.

If retailers were liable for all fraudulent costs after a breach, then there would be probably like a legal Fort Knox. And if payment networks were liable, there would be more robust security systems, as well. The point is that sometimes assigning blame, and in this case, assigning liablitity, is, in fact, important, because it incentivizes different parties to invest or not invest in fraud-reducing technology to protect consumers and our overall economy and it makes it more difficult for criminals.

So I really look forward to this hearing. I think it is incredibly important and I look forward to hearing of new innovations to protect identity and therefore, hopefully, our banking system.

Thank you very much. I yield back.

Chairwoman CAPITO. Thank you.

I recognize Mr. Pittenger for 2 minutes for an opening statement.

Mr. PITTENGER. Thank you, Chairwoman Capito, for allowing me to properly make this opening statement.

And thank you to each of the witnesses for coming today to testify.

We are here today to listen to experts from Homeland Security and the Secret Service and representatives of industry to learn about the ongoing effort to protect our fellow citizens' private information. We have seen over the past several years advancements in technology when Americans shop to pay for goods.

But with these new advancements certainly comes the responsibility of protecting the integrity of the system. As payment systems increasingly rely on electronic transmissions of personal financial data, Americans have a right and an expectation to know how that data is being protected, where it is stored, the extent to which the government has access to it, and the protocols that ought to be in place in private or public sector entities who mishandle, improperly disclose, or otherwise fail to ensure the security of personal financial information.

Over the last 6 months, several American companies and universities have experienced significant data breaches—my wife and I had a breach just yesterday—and while the details of these breaches remain under investigation by Federal and State law enforcement authorities, these episodes have disclosed a serious threat to financial privacy and data security posed by individuals and criminal syndicates.

We have to remain vigilant in our fight against these individuals and organizations. I know it is a difficult task to ask to be prepared to prevent 100 percent of the cyber attacks. But the consequences of not being equipped to handle the threat could ruin the lives and threaten the security of millions of Americans.

Thank you again for coming before the committee, and I look forward to hearing your testimony.

Chairwoman CAPITO. Thank you.

I would like to recognize Mr. Scott for 2 minutes for an opening statement.

Mr. SCOTT. Thank you very much, Madam Chairwoman. And this is indeed a very, very interesting and important hearing as more and more Americans shift to electronic payment systems and online shopping.

One of my professors at graduate school in economics and finance was an economist, John Kenneth Galbraith, and he produced a book about 40 years ago called, ''The New Industrial State.'' I bring that up because he made a very interesting statement. He said, ''Very shortly we in our country, and perhaps around the world, will soon become the victims and servants of the very machine that was created to serve us.''

I think we are at that point now. As payment systems increasingly rely on electronic transmission of personal financial data, Americans certainly have a right and an expectation to know how that data is protected. They need to know where it is stored, who has access to that data, and to what extent.

Americans have a right and an expectation to know the protocols that are and ought to be in place when entities, whether public or private, mishandle or improperly disclose or otherwise fail to ensure the security of their personal information.

We have the big picture here. We have to hold everybody accountable. Financial institutions must be held accountable to the same accountability as our retailers.

We have had over 110 million Americans impacted by this situation. Earlier, I had a very interesting conversation with one of our panelists, Mr. Troy Leach, and I think he is on to something here with the Security Standards Council. Perhaps we are indeed working on this, giving too much information, making too much information available, and that maybe we can cut down on some of that information so we don't make it so easy for hackers to access it.

I look forward to the hearing, Madam Chairwoman, and I yield back.

Chairwoman CAPITO. Thank you.

I now recognize the chairman emeritus of the full Financial Services Committee, Mr. Bachus, for 2 minutes for an opening statement.

Mr. BACHUS. Thank you, Madam Chairwoman.

One of Yogi Berra's most famous quotes is, "It is deja vu all over again." A little more than a decade ago, this committee investigated a series of data breaches involving New York City restaurants, cable companies, retail businesses of all kinds, banks, universities, and all branches of government from local to State to Federal. People's credit was being ruined, and their good names being used for criminal purposes. But identity theft suddenly became a national issue.

I remember this because I was chairman of the Financial Institutions Subcommittee at the time. I am proud of this committee because at the time, we held numerous hearings like the one today, that resulted in the Fair and Accurate Credit Transactions (FACT) Act or (FACTA), which was bipartisan legislation passed almost unanimously by this committee and signed into law by President Bush in December 2003.

The legislation created a number of protections, which I am convinced have helped prevent numerous cases of identity theft over the last 10 years. That is why your full credit card number is no longer on store or restaurant receipts, and you can place fraud alerts on your credit report. Very significantly, it is why consumers are entitled to be provided with free copies of their credit report from the three major reporting bureaus.

But I am having deja vu again because the same arguments that were being used then are being used again today against the adoption of marked chip and PIN cards. It won't be a total solution, and it wouldn't have prevented the Target breach, but it would prevent that information from then being used in credit transactions.

It wouldn't be a total solution. It wouldn't be easy. It would be complicated. It would be expensive. All of that is true. It was then, and it is now. But still, something needs to be done.

Let me close by saying, Mr. Noonan, you mentioned the National Computer Forensic Institute, and I want to compliment the Secret Service. They joined with the Alabama district attorney's office in the State of Alabama, Shelby County, and responded with that, and it has really helped, and I want to commend the Secret Service for that.

That building that it is housed in was donated by a county and a city in Birmingham—a modern facility at no cost to the taxpayers. And it is a way that we can inexpensively respond with innovative thinking. The people being trained there—it is in his testimony on page 8, and I commend you for mentioning that.

Thank you.

Chairwoman CAPITO. Thank you.

With that, I ask unanimous consent to allow members of the full Financial Services Committee who are not members of this subcommittee to sit in on today's hearing. Without objection, it is so ordered.

And with that, I would like to recognize Ms. Sinema for 1 minute for an opening statement.

Ms. SINEMA. Thank you, Madam Chairwoman.

And thank you, Ranking Member Meeks.

I believe that it is critical for public and private sector leaders to continue to push for the development of a strong cybersecurity industry that can protect our economic and national security interests. The nature of cyber means that nongovernment institutions and private sector companies alike need tools and resources to protect Americans' personal information from cyber attacks.

Several large companies such as Honeywell, Schwab, and America's Best have some or all of their security space in Arizona; and several smaller innovative companies like Bishop Fox and Securosis are among the significant and growing number of cybersecurity businesses in my home State.

Arizona is a hub for innovation. We are ahead of the curve on tech growth, thanks to entrepreneurial programs at Arizona State University, the University of Advancing Technology, and America's community colleges.

Thank you for the opportunity to highlight this critically important issue. Through your collaboration with government and innovative private institutions, I believe we can meet the cybersecurity challenges of today and tomorrow.

Thank you, Madam Chairwoman.

Chairwoman CAPITO. Thank you.

Mr. Green, for 2 minutes.

Mr. GREEN. Thank you, Madam Chairwoman. I will be pithy and concise. I would like to thank you for the hearing, and thank the ranking member, as well.

And I would like to, if I may, indicate to the public that while a hearing is titled, "Data Security: Examining Efforts to Protect Americans' Financial Information," the actual concern is much broader and much bigger. We are also concerned about medical information. We are also concerned about your travel history. We are concerned about the materials that you purchase—your reading materials.

This has implications that are far-reaching, that can have an impact on privacy beyond which we can't imagine currently. I am excited about the hearing and I am interested to find out how we can prevent this kind of encroachment on privacy.

I thank you, and I yield back.

Chairwoman CAPITO. The gentleman yields back.

All time has expired for opening statements, and I would like to welcome our first panel of distinguished witnesses. Each of you will be recognized for 5 minutes to give an oral presentation of your testimony. And without objection, each of your written statements will be made a part of the record.

Our first witness is Mr. William Noonan, Deputy Special Agent in Charge, Criminal Investigative Division, Cyber Operations Branch, United States Secret Service.

Welcome, Mr. Noonan.

STATEMENT OF WILLIAM NOONAN, DEPUTY SPECIAL AGENT IN CHARGE, CRIMINAL INVESTIGATIVE DIVISION, CYBER OPERATIONS BRANCH, UNITED STATES SECRET SERVICE

Mr. NOONAN. Good morning, Chairwoman Capito, Ranking Member Meeks, and distinguished members of the subcommittee. Thank you for the opportunity to testify on behalf of the Department of Homeland Security regarding the ongoing trend of criminals exploiting cyberspace to obtain sensitive financial and identity information as part of a complex criminal scheme to defraud our Nation's payment systems.

Our modern financial system depends heavily on information technology for convenience and efficiency. Accordingly, criminals motivated by greed have adapted their methods and are increasingly using cyberspace to exploit our Nation's financial payment systems to engage in fraud and other illicit activities.

The widely reported payment card data breaches of Target, Neiman Marcus, White Lodging, and other retailers are just recent examples of this trend. The Secret Service is investigating these recent data breaches and we are confident we will bring the criminals responsible to justice.

However, data breaches like these recent events are part of a long trend. In 1984, Congress recognized the risk posed by increasing use of information technology and established 18 USC Sections 1029 and 1030 through the Comprehensive Crime Control Act. These statutes define access device fraud and misuse of computers as Federal crimes and explicitly assign the Secret Service authority to investigate these crimes.

In support of the Department of Homeland Security's mission to safeguard cyberspace, the Secret Service has developed a unique record of success in investigating cyber crime through the efforts of our highly trained special agents and the work of our growing network of 35 electronic crimes task forces, which Congress assigned the mission of preventing, detecting, and investigating various forms of electronic crimes, including potential terrorist attacks against critical infrastructure and financial payment systems.

As a result of our cyber crime investigations, over the past 4 years the Secret Service has arrested nearly 5,000 cyber criminals. In total, these criminals were responsible for over $1 billion in fraud losses, and we estimate our investigations prevented over $11 billion in fraud losses.

Data breaches like the recently reported occurrences are just one part of a complex criminal scheme executed by organized cyber crime. These criminal groups are using increasingly sophisticated technology to conduct a criminal conspiracy consisting of five parts: one, gaining unauthorized access to computer systems carrying valuable, protected information; two, deploying specialized malware to capture and exfiltrate this data; three, distributing or selling this sensitive data to their criminal associates; four, engaging in sophisticated and distributed frauds using the sensitive information obtained; and five, laundering the proceeds of their illicit activity.

All five of these activities are criminal violations in and of themselves, and when conducted by sophisticated, transnational networks of cyber criminals, this scheme has yielded hundreds of millions of dollars in illicit proceeds.

The Secret Service is committed to protecting our Nation from this threat. We disrupt every step of their five-part criminal scheme through proactive criminal investigations and defeat these transnational cyber criminals through coordinated arrests and seizure of assets.

Foundational to these efforts are our private industry partners as well as our close partnerships with State, local, Federal, and international law enforcement. As a result of these partnerships, we were able to prevent many cyber crimes, by sharing criminal intelligence regarding the plans of cyber criminals and by working with the victim companies and financial institutions to minimize financial losses.

Through our Department's National Cybersecurity and Communications Integration Center, the NCCIC, the Secret Service also quickly shares technical cybersecurity information while protecting civil rights and civil liberties in order to enable other organizations to reduce their cyber risks by mitigating technical vulnerabilities.

We also partner with the private sector and academia to research cyber threats and public information on cyber crime trends through reports like the Carnegie Mellon CERT Insider Threat Study, the Verizon Data Breach Investigations Report, and the Trustwave Global Security Report.

The Secret Service has a long history of protecting our Nation's financial systems from threats. In 1865, the threat we were founded to address was that of counterfeit currency. As our financial payment system has evolved from paper, to plastic, and now digital information, so too has the investigative mission.

The Secret Service is committed to continuing to protect our Nation's financial system even as criminals increasingly exploit it through cyberspace. Through the dedicated efforts of our special agents, our electronic crimes task forces, and by working in close partnership with the Department of Justice—in particular, the computer crimes and intellectual property section—and local U.S. attorneys' offices, the Secret Service will continue to bring cyber criminals who perpetrate major data breaches to justice.

Thank you for the opportunity to testify on this important topic, and we look forward to your questions.

[The prepared statement of Deputy Special Agent in Charge Noonan can be found on page 84 of the appendix.]

Chairwoman CAPITO. Thank you.

Mr. Zelvin, you are recognized for 5 minutes.

STATEMENT OF LARRY ZELVIN, DIRECTOR, NATIONAL CYBERSECURITY AND COMMUNICATIONS INTEGRATION CENTER (NCCIC), U.S. DEPARTMENT OF HOMELAND SECURITY

Mr. ZELVIN. Chairwoman Capito, Ranking Member Meeks, and distinguished members of the subcommittee, thank you for the opportunity to appear before you today. In my brief opening comments, I would like to highlight the DHS National Cybersecurity and Communications Integration Center (NCCIC's) role in preventing, responding to, and mitigating cyber incidents, and then discuss our activities during the recent point-of-sale compromises.

As you well know, the Nation's economic vitality and national security depend on a secure cyberspace where reasonable risk decisions can be made on digital goods, transactions, and online interactions so that they can occur safely and reliably.

In order to meet this objective, we must share the technical characteristics of malicious cyber activity in a timely fashion so cyber defenders can discover, address, and mitigate information technology threats and vulnerabilities. It is increasingly clear that no single country, agency, company, or individual can effectively respond to the ever-rising threats of malicious cyber activity alone.

Effective responses require a whole-of-nation effort, including close coordination among entities like: DHS's NCCIC; the Secret Service; the Department of Justice, to include the Federal Bureau of Investigation; the intelligence community; sector-specific agencies, such as the Department of the Treasury; private sector entities, who are simply critical to these efforts; and State, local, tribal, territorial, and international governments. In carrying out our particular responsibilities, the NCCIC promotes and implements a unified approach to cybersecurity, which enables the efforts of bringing these diverse partners to quickly share cybersecurity information in a manner that ensures the protection of individuals' privacy, civil rights, and civil liberties.

As you may already know, the NCCIC is a civilian organization that provides an around-the-clock center where key government, private sector, and international partners can work together in both physical and virtual environments. The NCCIC is composed of four branches: the United States Computer Emergency Readiness Team, or US-CERT; the Industrial Control Systems CERT; the National Coordination Center for Communications; and Ops and Integration.

In response to the recent retailer compromises, the NCCIC specifically leveraged the resources and capabilities of US-CERT, whose mission focuses specifically on computer network defense, including prevention, protection, mitigation, and response activities. In executing this mission, the NCCIC and US-CERT regularly publish technical and nontechnical information products analyzing the characteristics of malicious cyber activities and improving the ability of organizations and individuals to reduce risk.

When appropriate, all NCCIC components have onsite response teams that can assist owners and operators at their facilities. In addition, US-CERT has global partnerships with over 200 CERTs worldwide that allow the teams to work directly with analysts across international borders.

Increasingly, data from the NCCIC and US-CERT can be shared in machine-readable formats, such as the Structured Threat Information Expression, also known as STIX, which is currently being implemented and utilized.

In the recent point-of-sale compromises NCCIC/US-CERT analyzed the malware provided to us by the Secret Service as well as other relevant technical data and used these findings, in part, to create a number of information-sharing products. The first, which is publicly available and can be found on the US-CERT Web site, provides a nontechnical overview of risks to point-of-sale systems along with recommendations on how businesses and individuals can better protect themselves and mitigate their losses in the event of an incident that has already occurred. Other products have been more limited in distribution and they are meant for cybersecurity professionals and provide technical analysis and mitigation recommendations to better enable expert-level protection, discovery, response, and recovery efforts.

As a matter of strategic intent, the NCCIC's goal is always to share information as broadly as possible. These efforts ensured that actionable details associated with major cyber events are shared with the right partners so they can protect themselves, their families, their businesses and organizations quickly and accurately.

In the case of the point-of-sale compromises, we especially benefited from the close coordination with the Financial Services Information Sharing and Analysis Center, or the FS-ISAC. In particular, the FS-ISAC's Payments Processing Information Sharing Council has been useful in that they provide a forum for sharing information about fraud, threats, vulnerabilities, and risk mitigation in the payments industry.

In conclusion, I want to highlight again that we in DHS and across the NCCIC strive every day to enhance the security and resilience across cyberspace and information technology enterprise. At every opportunity the NCCIC, in close coordination with our partners, publishes technical and nontechnical products to better enable our national critical infrastructure, businesses, and our citizens to protect against cyber threats, while also providing onsite technical assistance whenever necessary.

We will accomplish our mission through voluntary means, ever mindful of the need to respect privacy, civil liberties, and the law. I truly appreciate the opportunity to speak with you today and look forward to your questions.

[The prepared statement of Mr. Zelvin can be found on page 95 of the appendix.]

Chairwoman CAPITO. Thank you.

And I am offering my sincere apologies to you, as the first panel, and to the next panel, and to the members of this subcommittee, but we are going to call a recess subject to the call of the Chair. We expect it to be a half hour, so that would be 11:05; hopefully, we can call back in sooner.

Again, I apologize.

[recess]

Chairwoman CAPITO. I am going to go ahead and reconvene the hearing. Thank you for your patience.

Mr. Meeks will be here in a few minutes, but I am going to go ahead and begin my questioning so we can move along a little bit.

Mr. Noonan, in your statement you mentioned that the Secret Service had either arrested or gotten 5,000 criminals. Was that the number that you used?

Mr. NOONAN. Yes, ma'am.

Chairwoman CAPITO. Those, I assume, are all American citizens in the United States? Because we hear about how a lot of this is occurring offshore. Are you coordinating in any international fashion, or—if you could just kind of give me a little background on that?

Mr. NOONAN. Sure, ma'am. That figure comprises all of the cases that we have made arrests on that have any connection back to the use of cyber in those crimes.

So to say that they are domestic or international, it is both.

Chairwoman CAPITO. It is both.

Mr. NOONAN. Yes. We have a very unique success of bringing international, transnational cyber criminals to justice here domestically, but that figure that we have provided for you there is domestic and international.

Chairwoman CAPITO. Okay.

Mr. Zelvin, you are from Homeland Security, and Mr. Noonan is with the Secret Service. I think sometimes we find that when there is coordination between Federal agencies, who is in charge, I guess is always a good question. I know it is a collaborative effort, but who is really leading this in your mind, from your agency's perspective?

Mr. ZELVIN. Yes, ma'am. It is a team effort so there is a variety, depending on which area you are looking at. As you are looking at the law enforcement aspect, the Secret Service and the Federal Bureau of Investigation have the primacy, depending on the cyber case. When you look at the intelligence field, obviously the National Security Agency, the Central Intelligence Agency, and others have primacy, whether you are talking about electronics intelligence or human intelligence.

We at the NCCIC specifically really focus on those network defense measures—understanding the intrusions, understanding how to plug those holes, and then preventing them from reoccurring. We have the responsibility, as well, of protecting the Federal dot-gov space, and that is a big part of our effort, and then we work across the private sector at 16 critical infrastructures, and as I mentioned in my opening statement, the international partnerships.

Chairwoman CAPITO. Mr. Noonan, would you concur with Mr. Zelvin in terms of who is in charge or the coordinative aspect of what you are doing? I know we talk a lot about coordination, and both of you did in your statements, but I am trying to make sure that if Mr. Meeks and I say we are both in charge, but then something goes wrong, and I say, "But he was in charge," so—

Mr. NOONAN. Yes, for sure. In an investigation like this law enforcement generally takes charge of the investigative piece—

Chairwoman CAPITO. Right.

Mr. NOONAN. —and information-sharing we do through a bunch of different mechanisms. Our primary source for information-sharing is through the NCCIC, but we also partner, as well, with the FS-ISAC. Obviously, the Secret Service has a rich history of working in the financial services sector.

Chairwoman CAPITO. Right.

Mr. NOONAN. So the FS-ISAC, who is going to be on the next panel, is another great partner that we use to push information out to the financial services sector.

In addition to that, we have 35 electronic crimes task forces. And those electronic crimes task forces that we have aren't just made up of law enforcement; they are made up of the private sector, so we have members from the private sector working side by side with agents, where we share information back and forth, as well as academia. So that is another method that the Secret Service uses to push information that is going to better protect the private industry and the critical infrastructure that we have.

Chairwoman CAPITO. When there is a data breach from a retailer, say, such as what happened with Target—and I know the investigation is ongoing so not specifically that, I am just using it as an example—is the way that you are made aware of this through individuals whose cards have been corrupted, or does the company itself, whatever company it is, is it incumbent upon them to come to you? How does that reach your level of understanding of what is going on?

Mr. NOONAN. It depends on the case, ma'am. I brought up in my oral remarks that we have a proactive approach to law enforcement. And there is a reactive approach, in which the crime has already occurred, and we are chasing the clues back to the criminal to identify who the criminal is to affect an arrest.

Chairwoman CAPITO. Right.

Mr. NOONAN. The proactive approach of what we do in law enforcement is we are out working with sources, we are out working undercover operations, we are working with private sector banking investigators, and in our proactive approach there are many times where we identify a potential breach before it has occurred. And we find that it is more valuable—it is critical for law enforcement, then, to make notification to that industry, to that private sector partner, to be able to stop the crime from occurring.

Chairwoman CAPITO. Okay. Let me stop you there because I am running out of time, but I am curious to know, in the case of a retailer where this could have an effect on their future sales, do you find that they are willing to make this breach public and really better inform everybody who could be affected by such a breach?

Mr. NOONAN. Again, it depends on the company—

Chairwoman CAPITO. Right.

Mr. NOONAN. —and it depends on the case, so—

Chairwoman CAPITO. Yes.

Mr. NOONAN. —I can't give you a yes-or-no answer.

Chairwoman CAPITO. Right. You can see both sides of it. I would think more and more it is in the company's best interest, obviously, to be as open and transparent as possible in something of this nature.

Mr. Meeks?

Mr. MEEKS. Thank you, Madam Chairwoman.

Let me start with Mr. Noonan, and let me maybe ask a question that might not even be fair because I am going to ask you how to help me do my job. You urge Congress to take legislative action that could help to improve the Nation's cybersecurity, reduce regulatory costs on U.S. companies, and strengthen law enforcement's ability to conduct effective investigations. I think that was part of your testimony.

And, I am sure that all parties agree with this in general, when you make the general assessment, but there are differing, at times, interests, and sometimes even competing interests that individuals would have. For example, there may be different interests between card issuers, merchants, and consumers. They can all overlap, but ultimately there could be divergent visions of how the government can best solve these problems.

So, we are going to be trying to dig into this and talking to a number of different folks, but I would like to get your opinion. How would you suggest as lawmakers we balance these interests and create a plan that can satisfy the core concerns of all parties? Because we have this balancing act that we have to do but we need to—we want to help you also, so how would you suggest we do that?

Mr. NOONAN. Yes, sir. So from the law enforcement perspective—and that is what I can provide to you—I think it is important and it is critical for companies that have been exposed, companies that have knowledge of a potential breach, to bring that to law enforcement's attention. Law enforcement, at that point, is critical in the fact that it can, obviously, collect evidence to try to make a difference, make a physical arrest of a criminal. But I think it is also important that at that point in time, is when the information-sharing piece begins. Because if law enforcement is brought in early and we are able to draw the cybersecurity concerns out of the investigation, the evidence out of that, and we are able to take that information, we are able to minimize that information and protect the victim. We are able to then share that information with my partners over at the NCCIC and get that out to the greater infrastructure of this Nation so that they can better protect themselves from an additional potential attack to other pieces or other avenues of infrastructure.

Mr. MEEKS. Should the notification that goes out to you, go out to the consumer or the customer at the same time? For example, I was just wondering how long do most companies wait before they even notify you and/or notify the customer that their sensitive personal information may have been breached.

Mr. NOONAN. I would agree, sir. I think that it should be in a short period of time that the information should be put out to the customers. I, too, fell victim to a data breach as well, where it was inconvenient for myself and my family. So I think I am able to better respond as a customer to help support my family, but I think there is also a law enforcement concern there, as well, where there are situations and there are points in time wherein law enforcement may or may not need a window of opportunity to run operations to determine what has happened or who is behind the effort or the attack.

Mr. MEEKS. Let me just also, in that regard, ask Mr. Zelvin a question. I know in your testimony you also talked about the various virtual currencies as a means of laundering illicit proceeds, and I was wondering whether or not the Secret Service or other regulators have taken any action to address some of those concerns? And in your view, do regulators have—do you have sufficient authority to address the risk that these currencies pose as identified in your testimony?

Mr. NOONAN. Yes, sir. Just as early as last year the Secret Service, along with HSI and IRS, was successful in taking down a virtual currency or a digital currency called Liberty Reserve. Liberty Reserve was one of those digital currencies which the criminal underground used in which they would launder their money anonymously, and we were effective in taking that marketplace out of the criminal underground, as well as we were able and successful in arresting the people who were behind the setup of that operation.

So it is more important than just taking the operation off, but we also arrested the people behind it.

Mr. MEEKS. Thank you.

Really quick, Mr. Zelvin, what about individual criminal activity outside of the United States? What can be done to go after these illicit actors? And what tools do you have to ensure that foreign individuals are also held accountable? Does that fit within our—

Mr. ZELVIN. Ranking Member Meeks, that is a question I would recommend for the FBI and the Secret Service—I will talk from the US-CERT perspective. We work with 200 like-minded CERTs around the world. We are in contact with them in many cases on a weekly basis and we are able to work our mitigations. I was in London about 3 weeks ago, and when we were meeting with our counterparts, they said the point-of-sale product that we had from US-CERT was very helpful to them because they were bringing it to their industries, because what had happened here in the United States they felt was probably happening in the U.K. and around Europe, and this was instructive for them, as well.

Mr. MEEKS. Thank you.

Chairwoman CAPITO. Thank you.

Mr. Pearce?

Mr. PEARCE. Thank you, Madam Chairwoman.

I appreciate both of the witnesses being here. Mr. Rothfus and I have decided we are going to cut up our cards right here among us while we are listening to you, so if you have any scissors, pass them on up.

Mr. Zelvin, has the CFPB called you all? Are you all working with them in any way?

Mr. ZELVIN. Congressman, the CFPB?

Mr. PEARCE. Yes.

Mr. ZELVIN. The Consumer Financial Protection Bureau?

Mr. PEARCE. Yes.

Mr. ZELVIN. No, we haven't been in contact with them directly.

Mr. PEARCE. Mr. Noonan?

Mr. NOONAN. No, sir.

Mr. PEARCE. No. They are collecting 990 million records. Target lost 40 million. They are collecting 990 million. It seems like they would be calling the Nation's best to say, "What do we do for data security?" Amazing.

What kind of protection is available against a Snowden-type attack? In other words, he is working inside and pulls those records, downloads a three-mile-high stack of records, and is there any protection?

Either one of you?

Mr. NOONAN. From the Federal Government standpoint, when we are talking about retail-type positions, there is nothing that we have that would stop an insider threat.

Mr. PEARCE. I guess I didn't make it clear. The CFPB is—would be parallel to the NSA. I don't want to carry that analogy too far, but they are a government agency and they are collecting a massive amount of data—massive—almost a billion credit cards. And so I guess I am interested in if somebody inside the agency wants to release documents, like Mr. Snowden was inside the agency, it wasn't planned, and the agency didn't approve of it, so is there any protection for the Snowden-type attack from inside the agencies?

Mr. ZELVIN. Congressman, I can answer the question broadly, not specifically. So broadly, the insider threat is one of the most difficult things we face. I think the one that is probably almost as bad is if somebody was into what we call the supply chain.

The ability to defend against the insider threat is developing quickly but we are not where we need to be by a long shot. There are things in the financial community which are leading the way that we are taking as lessons, but as you rightly point out, it is a vulnerability and a weakness that we need to get better on, and we need to do so quickly.

Mr. PEARCE. Okay.

Mr. Noonan, your testimony had some numbers in it, but I don't know that I saw the scope. In other words, I saw 4,900—that is the people that we had—that you have had 4,900 arrests. What is the scope? How many cyber attacks are there each day, roughly?

Mr. NOONAN. I can't comment on the number of attacks that occur every day.

Mr. PEARCE. Because it is too secret, or you just don't know?

Mr. NOONAN. No, we don't compile our data in that manner. We have active investigations, so—

Mr. PEARCE. What would you guess? Hundreds of thousands a day? Is that too high?

Mr. NOONAN. I think there are cyber criminals who are probing our systems every day. I think every moment, they are probing our systems.

Mr. PEARCE. Yes, every day, hundreds of thousands, and I suspect that your agency is probably strained for resources. To put it in perspective, in your testimony you talk about the 11 that you have indicted; how many convictions have you been able to get through the system?

Mr. NOONAN. Numerous convictions. We have had—

Mr. PEARCE. Numerous. How many? Like 20,000?

Mr. NOONAN. No, sir.

Mr. PEARCE. 22,000? What is numerous?

Mr. NOONAN. I would say that it is in the range of several hundred a year.

Mr. PEARCE. Several hundred. In the paragraph right above where you are talking about the 11, you are talking about how one system has 80,000 users. That is an illicit system—80,000 users and we are getting 11. That is absolutely frightening, the scope that is coming at us and the system is, again, very difficult to work in, with almost no protections against inside attacks where people knowingly download and give away information.

Snowden gave away, again, 1.8 million documents, and I just—I worry the CFPB has not even talked to you. Mr. Cordray got somewhat offended at the line of questioning and began to rewrite the question. I didn't accuse him of—going to do it, I just said that any agency—this information is widely viewable by almost everybody in the agency and widely accessible, and yet they haven't even called the best people in the Nation.

I would recommend that the next time we have the CFPB come in and sit down and talk about the protections, maybe they have better operations than these two guys were able to present, but I find it stunning that they have not even contacted either one of you.

Thank you. I yield back.

Mr. LUETKEMEYER [presiding]. Thank you.

Now, the Chair recognizes the gentlelady from New York, Mrs. Maloney.

Mrs. MALONEY. Thank you so much. And I feel this is an incredible challenge for our country. Just talking to four friends on the panel, all four of us have had our identity stolen. The fact that 40 billion people lost their—40 million, I guess it was, from Target. That is staggering.

So the cost to individuals, law enforcement, and institutions is absolutely huge. One of the problems I see is that the reaction time is so slow. By the time we put something in place, say the data breach chip by 2015, the hackers will have gone on to the next stage of how to hack that.

And it seems to me the next phase is going to be online. Most of the transactions are online. So the tokenism idea and technology seems the most promising to me.

When you do find a breach, Mr. Noonan, and you said that you are sometimes the first to notice it—who do you notify? Do you notify the financial institution, the consumer, or the retailer, or all three? What do you when you notice a breach? What do you do?

Mr. NOONAN. It depends on who the victim is, ma'am. If it is a retailer, we would obviously contact the security department of that retailer and we would suggest to them different steps to look at their system to be able to determine if, in fact—

Mrs. MALONEY. Okay. Do you tell them to also notify the bank and notify the consumer? Who does—

Mr. NOONAN. Yes, ma'am.

Mrs. MALONEY. Okay.

Mr. NOONAN. So the part we would do is we would have them work closely with the financial institutions and the processing system which they use.

Mrs. MALONEY. Now you also said that—and also retailers have said—that the reason that they don't immediately disclose a data breach is that public disclosure would hinder law enforcement efforts to catch the criminal. Is that true?

Mr. NOONAN. Not in all cases, ma'am.

Mrs. MALONEY. And why would public disclosure hinder an investigation?

Mr. NOONAN. Just at a point in time where there was potentially an undercover operation, it could hamper the conclusion of that undercover operation. So the time that we are talking is a very small window of time.

Mrs. MALONEY. I believe most public policy and resources are directed when we have good data, so who is keeping the data on how big a problem it is in the United States? It is huge in terms of the national security and financial security and economic security of our country.

Somebody has to be tracking the overall picture of the extent and the depth of it and the techniques. Who is doing that if the CIA is not doing it? Who is doing the overall—we have to be collecting that data in a broad way to analyze trends and movements.

Who is collecting that data? Somebody has to be collecting it. If they aren't, then someone should be. Who is collecting that data—the FBI, the CIA, Homeland Security?

Mr. ZELVIN. Congresswoman, let me answer the question this way: We are all collecting data in areas in which we have the ability to see the information.

Mrs. MALONEY. Okay, but then who is getting the overall picture for our national security and economic security?

Mr. ZELVIN. Again, it is being looked at by Homeland Security. We in the NCCIC look at the overall picture. But it is a matter of looking at the Internet service providers, and managed security service providers, and others, and taking that data and aggregating it.

But I will tell you that we still don't have the visibility on everything. It is still just a snapshot. But those snapshots are useful because they show trends and then our ability to provide mitigations.

So if you look at these security reports that Mr. Noonan has here, they will talk about things like spearphishing and man-in-the-middle attacks and all these other things, and we are defending against those things, so we have a lot of work to do as we take this data to build security measures so they are not successful. But that aggregation, it doesn't exist; we are just compiling data from a lot of sources.

Mrs. MALONEY. Before 9/11, we had 18 different intelligence organizations working independently, not sharing their information. The most important reform was that we created the Department of Homeland Security and combined all of our intelligence so we are working in a coordinated way.

We have to do the same thing with cybersecurity. Somebody has to be in charge of the overall picture.

And I know everybody is doing a good job in their department, and I would say the private sector is doing a pretty good job, too. Who is coordinating with finding the top things the private sector is doing with the top things the government is doing?

This is a number one national security issue; it is not just an economic issue. And so, who is doing that? Is it Homeland Security? Somebody has to be pulling it all together. Who is in charge of doing that?

Mr. ZELVIN. Congresswoman, I will tell you, I think it is our responsibility at the NCCIC, as you describe it, to bring that all together, especially on the network defense side—so to be able to work with the private sector; to work with the critical infrastructure sectors; to work with State, local, tribal, territorial; to work with our international partners. That is what we are doing on a daily basis.

Last year alone, the Center had 240,000 cyber incidents reported to us. But again, that is probably a fraction of the greater whole. But our numbers are increasing upwards at about 60 percent a year as far as—

Mrs. MALONEY. And is the private sector also sending you their information?

Mr. ZELVIN. Yes, Congresswoman, they are, but it is done on a voluntary basis. They have no requirement to do so. The Federal Government has requirements to report to US-CERT under policy and other requirements, but the private sector reporting is voluntary and that is why one of the initiatives that has been asked for is the data breach reporting requirement.

Mrs. MALONEY. Okay. Thank you.

Mr. LUETKEMEYER. I thank the gentlelady.

With that, it is my turn to ask the questions, so the Chair now allows himself 5 minutes to engage the witnesses, as well.

I want to follow up on Mr. Pearce's comments with regards to the CFPB. I was kind of stunned, taken aback that you gentleman hadn't heard of or weren't aware of the CFPB, and I would certainly echo the concerns of Mr. Pearce from the standpoint that in committee, they actually testified themselves that they have access and take in at least 80 percent of the credit card transactions per day that occur in this country.

That sort of access, that sort of accumulation of data in one agency is, quite frankly, scary. You are looking at what happened with Target and Neiman Marcus and some of the other merchants, and now you have a government agency that has 80 percent of all the credit card transactions going on in this country on a daily basis accumulating in their files and they are not coordinating with each of you? That certainly scares the dickens out of me, so I would certainly urge you to contact those folks and see once if there is a way that you can coordinate with them to see if there is something that they find which needs to be checked out.

With that, I was curious—I assume that you have jurisdiction to go to any individual company or group or industry, whatever, if there is a challenge or some sort of a cyber breakdown within that group that deals with personal information. Is that correct?

Mr. NOONAN. The authority to go actually into the organization itself?

Mr. LUETKEMEYER. Yes.

Mr. NOONAN. We would use the court process to be able to work with that company so—

Mr. LUETKEMEYER. Okay.

Mr. NOONAN. —if somebody was reluctant or there was a company that was reluctant, we could potentially use the court process to do that, sir.

Mr. LUETKEMEYER. The reason I asked the question is that when—we are talking mostly this morning about financial institutions and merchants, but there are other entities out there that have personal information, sometimes have monetary transactions that occur. One of the things, for instance, you are looking at different kinds of, for instance, schools, associations—I kind of made a list here of other groups—hospitals—medical information is huge these days, as well as credit bureaus.

So have you taken any actions or coordinated with any of those kind of groups before with regards to this?

Mr. NOONAN. Yes, sir. Again, through our electronic crimes task forces, we would partnering with those different institutions, as well.

We go after any sort of cyber criminal which is seeking to benefit through the monetization of whatever that they are trying to accomplish or steal. So in many of these situations that you have brought up, personally identifiable information is a piece that is of great concern to us, which the criminal underground can monetize and gain from.

So any opportunity that we can work with a potential victim company before it occurs or as it has occurred to be able to go at those cyber criminals who are—

Mr. LUETKEMEYER. One of the reasons I bring that up is a lot of those folks, for instance, are not as aware of the ability of somebody to get into their records because they probably don't deal with financial matters as much. But yet, they are probably more at risk than anybody else because their systems probably aren't protected as well as, I would think, for instance, financial institutions. So, just kind of an observation.

One of the questions I also had was, what about penalties? Do you guys ever catch anybody? How many folks have you caught in the last 5 years?

Mr. NOONAN. As a matter of fact, yes. I am talking about international, the higher-level cyber criminals.

Going back, starting in 2005, the Secret Service successfully arrested Roman Vega out of the Ukraine. He was sentenced to 18 years, sir. In 2008, out of Estonia, Alexander Suvorov was sentenced to 7 years. In 2010, Russian Israeli citizen Vladislav Horohorin received 88 months, and Igor Shevelev, a citizen of the Ukraine, was sentenced to 13 to 40 years in New York.

Mr. LUETKEMEYER. Are they serving time in the United States?

Mr. NOONAN. They are serving time here domestically, sir.

Mr. LUETKEMEYER. They sound like they are all—and you indicated they are all from foreign countries—

Mr. NOONAN. They are all international, transnational—

Mr. LUETKEMEYER. Okay.

Mr. NOONAN. —cyber criminals that we were able to successfully arrest internationally, and have extradited back to the United States where they are serving their sentences domestically here in the United States—

Mr. LUETKEMEYER. Now, are there other tools or other things that you need to be able to do your job better or to have better access to be able to bring charges against individuals? Is there something we need to do to help you do your job better?

Mr. NOONAN. Sir, what we are doing, which is bringing great success in the arena of going after international cyber criminals, is our partnerships with our international law enforcement partners as well as the international offices that we have and the international working groups that we have overseas. Because cyber crime knows no borders, we think it is important to be working outside of our own borders and developing these partnerships.

So anything that we can get—continue to grow in the area of our international partnerships is where we find value right now in bringing these targets to justice.

Mr. LUETKEMEYER. Okay. Thank you.

My time has expired.

Mr. NOONAN. Thank you.

Mr. LUETKEMEYER. With that, we will recognize the ranking member of the full Financial Services Committee, Ms. Waters.

Ms. WATERS. Thank you very much. And I ask unanimous consent to submit my opening statement for the record.

Mr. LUETKEMEYER. Without objection, it is so ordered.

Ms. WATERS. I would like to thank our witnesses for being here today. We are also very interested in this subject, and I think that there was a bipartisan effort to support this hearing.

I would like to know, in light of the fact that the intrusion of Target came through a set of compromised vendor credentials, what, if any, updated guidance is being given to companies to heighten their due diligence of vendors to ensure they are, in fact, legitimate actors?

Mr. NOONAN. So surrounding the information of the potential—of the attacks that have occurred over the past several months, as we learn information on those attacks we are able to learn what criminal tools the perpetrators are utilizing. We take that information, and we analyze that information with the help of the NCCIC, and the NCCIC is the main operation that sends out the information to other industry.

It is also partnered closely with the FS-ISAC, which is the Financial Services Information Sharing and Analysis Center, to take the information learned and push the tactics and trends of what is happening out to industry. And Mr. Zelvin could probably comment a little bit more on exactly how they are doing that.

Mr. ZELVIN. Yes, ma'am. We got the malware, or the malicious software, from the Secret Service. We analyzed it.

We actually put out three different products. Informational products—the first one went to law enforcement so they could go out and hopefully find the actors who did this. The second one was a more technical product that went out to cyber defenders not only at the financial services companies and the retailers but also to the cyber defense community, managed security service providers, and Internet service providers, but the people who really understand one-zeros and backslashes and hashtags. Lastly, we have on the US-CERT Web site for consumers and the general population guidance on what they can do to protect themselves, and if they have been a victim, what they can do to recover from these events.

Ms. WATERS. So you do have some specific vendor information so that these companies can make a decision about whether or not they are credible vendors?

Mr. ZELVIN. Yes, ma'am. The government has put out information, the Financial Services ISAC has put out information, and also, the industry writ large is working hard at the problem. So, it is being attacked from a number of areas.

Internationally, I will tell you we have gotten some focus there in working with our partners, because this is a global problem, not just a U.S. problem.

Ms. WATERS. I would like to ask Mr. Noonan a question about Attorney General Eric Holder's recent urging of Congress to establish a national standard for notifying Americans of data breaches in light of the theft, of course, of customer data at Target and other major retailers. Would you support a national breach notification standard? And if so, do you have any specific recommendations for how that should be crafted?

I heard what you just said about all the things that are being done, but I think what is being urged by Attorney General Holder is a little bit different. Are you familiar with that? And what do you think?

Mr. NOONAN. Yes, ma'am. The Secret Service does support any initiative which would bring a data breach to the attention of a law enforcement agency with jurisdiction to be able to help bring criminals to justice and also to help in the aid of information-sharing.

Ms. WATERS. So you would consider that Congress does not need to establish a national standard for notifying Americans of data breaches? I appreciate that you have come up with some ways to approach this, including the notification of Americans, but there is nothing in law where we have set a standard.

Do you think Congress should do that or could be helpful to you in doing that? Would you want to put something like that together as a recommendation for us to place in law?

Mr. NOONAN. Yes. Absolutely.

Ms. WATERS. Okay. Mr. Zelvin?

Mr. ZELVIN. Ma'am, I would absolutely agree. Last year at the Center, we had 240,000 incidents reported, but we know that is only a fraction of what is actually happening out there. There is no requirement.

We would be supportive of that. We think it should be a public-private discussion to build what is the most appropriate way to come up with that standard, but we would support it.

Ms. WATERS. Thank you so very much.

Mr. Chairman, I yield back the balance of my time.

Mr. LUETKEMEYER. Thank you.

With that, we recognize the gentleman from Alabama, the chairman emeritus of the full Financial Services Committee, Mr. Bachus, for 5 minutes.

Mr. BACHUS. I thank the gentleman from Missouri.

The Target incident has focused a lot of attention on data breaches at the point of sale, and I will ask Mr. Noonan, does the National Computer Forensic Institute (NCFI) have experience with these type of cases, and are there any lessons we can draw or any successful prosecutions?

Mr. NOONAN. Yes, sir. NCFI is an operation where the Secret Service brings State and locals to understand cyber crime the same way that Secret Service understands cyber crime.

We teach them computer forensics; we teach them network intrusion capabilities; we teach them cell phone forensics, as well, and a litany of other courses to bring State and local law enforcement to the same level of understanding of cyber crime as the Secret Service. We utilize that facility as a capacity-building to help local law enforcement understand and be able to go after the small and medium-sized compromises, as well.

A great success that we have out of the NCFI is a case in which a national restaurant chain was compromised in the same way that Target was compromised, through a POS case—intrusion case. Our office in Manchester, New Hampshire, worked this case and they worked it with the support of State and local law enforcement. And it was the State and local law enforcement that we were able to train at NCFI in understanding the forensics that were going on that actually were critical in bringing, in that case, three international, transnational cyber criminals to justice.

So it is a force multiplication effort of the Secret Service, by training State and local law enforcement that are in your communities to have the same level of training, the same level of tools that the Secret Service has to go after these types of criminals.

Not to mention that State and locals can't use that same equipment and that same training to do other types of cyber crime that is important to them in their communities, as well. So we know that agents or officers that we have trained and detectives that we have trained have also used those skills to bring homicide suspects to justice, pedophile suspects to justice, and a litany of other suspects.

It doesn't stop at State and local law enforcement. We also have trained numerous State and local prosecutors as well as judges at that facility. So in the past 4 years, we have trained over 2,000 State and local members there.

Mr. BACHUS. Let me ask both of you this question, and it really goes into what Congresswoman Waters was saying: With Target, they delayed announcing anything until a blogger basically put on his blog that there had been a security breach, and then they disclosed the 40 million on their debit cards. But I think, Mr. Zelvin, you may have referred to this, they didn't report the 70 million on the personally identifiable information, which actually is almost a worse problem than the credit or the debit cards, because you can change the debit card. They didn't change the PPIs, and it is pretty hard to change your address or your grandmother's maiden name or the community you were born in, which are all used for passwords, so, there was all kinds of information. You are probably not going to change your phone number, and so those things are pretty difficult.

And there has been a lot of discussion, and I have advocated before for some uniform Federal standard for disclosing this information—who you disclose it to and the timeframe. Because right now, they operate under—it depends on what State, and the disclosure laws are all different in different States.

So if you would like to address the need for a—what we will call a uniform Federal standard?

Mr. ZELVIN. Congressman, I think one of the better examples is on the Federal side, the dot-gov side, the Federal departments and agencies, at least in the Executive Branch. You have a requirement to report if you had an intrusion, if you had a denial of service, if you have had a number of cyber events. That doesn't exist outside the dot-gov domain.

So it really is incumbent upon that company to decide what they want to do and how they want to do it, and I know they talk about it at the highest levels, they bring in their security professionals who bring their attorneys, and then there is a decision made and the decision is either to disclose or not to disclose. They have to make a risk management decision of whether or not it is better to say something.

I think we would—what I worry about is someday there could be that cyber 9/11, Pearl Harbor, whatever your analogy is, and the Congress will be asking, "What do you need?" This will be top on our list because if we don't know, we can't help to protect and secure the Nation.

Mr. BACHUS. Mr. Noonan?

Mr. NOONAN. Yes, sir. I would agree that a lot of times companies have to make a decision based on—they do make a decision based on a business need as opposed to what is right for the victim.

Mr. BACHUS. Right.

Thank you.

Chairwoman CAPITO. The gentleman's time has expired.

Mr. Scott?

Mr. SCOTT. Thank you very much.

In light of everything that has happened, do each of you believe that our retailers are held accountable and responsible for cybersecurity at the same standard and level as our financial institutions?

Mr. ZELVIN. Congressman, let me answer your question this way: We don't have national standards; we are building them now. That is part of the President's Executive Order and—forgive me—let me make sure I get the name right—there is the Cyber Critical Infrastructure Community Voluntary Program, the C3 program.

Mr. SCOTT. But don't our financial institutions have standards now? My point is that, are the retailers held to that same level as our financial institutions? Because quite honestly, if not, much of what we are doing here is in vain: 110 million Americans have suffered mainly because, in my humble opinion, retailers are not held to as high a standard in this issue as the financial institutions, and it is critical that we get those two on the same page quickly.

Mr. ZELVIN. Agreed, sir. The standards can be legislated; they can be put out by regulators; they can be enforced by the industry themselves. And I think your point is there are certain places in industry where they don't have standards and it would be very helpful to do so.

Mr. SCOTT. Let's talk about that for a moment because, as you notice from the questions from our committee, we are eager here in Congress to respond to this issue. This is almost like a Poseidon tidal wave coming at us.

As you rightly point out in your testimony, there are now over 2 billion Internet users. There are over 12 billion computers and other instruments that are used, and satellite devices, and so forth. And in the next 10 years that is estimated to possibly double.

So the issue becomes, can we win this? Can we with this battle? That is especially true because not only—even if we just existed over the next 10 years at the same level of sophistication of these technical devices, which we have become sort of servants to instead of servants to us.

So the question becomes, with the rapid advancements in technology—just think: Ten years ago, we didn't have what we have now, and what we have now, my God, is going to be ancient 10 years from now and we are going to have double the people with it. So I think the American people are looking for some confidence here that their vital security is at stake, and then more than that, the Nation's security is at stake.

Let me ask you an interesting question, Mr. Noonan. What was very interesting about your comment, because I wanted to get to—you said you caught some people and you mentioned sentencing of these people. Are there any possibilities for parole in this or negotiation or anything like that?

Mr. NOONAN. In the Federal system, my understanding is that there can be downward departures of sentences, but not that I know of as—

Mr. SCOTT. That is interesting. Why so? Because you see, these national conspiracies, as you so aptly put it, are very sophisticated. And it could be that they are even more sophisticated than you or us or where we are.

So why are there plea agreements? Why don't we have stiff, hard criminal sanctions and put these folks who do wrong in jail for what they are doing to the country?

The other point I wanted to ask is that you mentioned that all of these were foreigners attacking us. Now, that begs the question, why aren't they attacking—I don't want them to attack France or Germany or Great Britain—but the question is, why us? Is there something that these other nations are doing that deters them, and we are vulnerable where other nations aren't? Is that a possibility, since the only ones that you have been able to get ahold of and put away, hopefully for a while, are foreigners?

Mr. NOONAN. Sir, we know that these cyber criminals are not just attacking the United States. This is a global issue. This is not just a national issue to the United States; this is a global issue.

These particular criminals are attacking wherever they can find wealth and monetize that data.

Mr. SCOTT. How are we doing compared to these other nations? Are these other nations putting them away as they should? Is there coordination with other nations?

Mr. NOONAN. Yes, sir. We are coordinating very closely with other nations. And to be honest, we have a very, very rich success rate of getting some significant, stiff sentences.

Albert Gonzalez was a domestic target that we arrested in the TJX and Heartland Payment Systems breach. He was sentenced to 20 years in prison here in the United States.

We also have a litany of other huge sentences. I brought up earlier Roman Vega out of the Ukraine was sentenced to 18 years in prison. Recently, out of Romania, Mr. Oprea was sentenced to 15 years in prison here domestically for, again, point-of-sale breaches we are talking about today.

Chairwoman CAPITO. The gentleman's time—

Mr. SCOTT. And the national breach law is what you recommend we do?

Mr. NOONAN. Yes, sir.

Mr. SCOTT. Okay.

Chairwoman CAPITO. Thank you.

Mr. Stutzman?

Mr. STUTZMAN. Thank you, Madam Chairwoman.

And I thank both of the witnesses for being here today.

I would like to follow up just a little bit on the questions that you just talked about in, I guess, retailers. I come from a small business background and have small business—or a retail small business as well, and obviously any sort of credit card is a convenience for both consumer and for the retailer, but the role that retailers play—granted, I am small, but there are large retailers out there. Can you share with us a little bit of what—how is that data stored? Do they keep that data?

For us, we don't—we have no interest in it other than the transaction, and so I guess I am trying to follow up and understand why would we expect the retailers to be held to a different standard—or at the same standard as the financial institutions? Is there an effort out there by retailers even trying to do that?

I guess I would be concerned about that to some extent, because the more information that is held in different groups' hands, the more opportunity there is going to be for breaches. I don't know if either of you had a comment on that?

Mr. NOONAN. Yes, sir. Actually on your next panel you have a witness from PCI who is going to be able to discuss some of those issues, but regulations have changed over the course of the years, so back in 2005, TJX intrusion happened where cyber criminals were able to go after a database where retailers were able to, at that time, store credit card data unencrypted in servers. So, the criminals were able to exfiltrate a whole database of stored credit card data in 2005.

Because of that intrusion, industry changed. No longer can you store credit card data on a database within your system.

So what the criminals then did is they looked at, where is the path of least resistance, and they attacked Heartland Payment Systems, which was a credit card processing company. Credit card data during that period of time crossed over the system from the retailer to the credit card processing company to the bank, and in that system it was not encrypted data during that period of time.

Again, after that intrusion happened, the standards changed and from point to point credit card data and data information had to be encrypted.

Today, the criminals are going after, again, where is the edge of the fence? So, they have gone after the point-of-sale systems.

In domestic retail shops, from the point that you swipe your credit card at the terminal, that data goes to a back-of-the-house server, to a computer in the back that you see it, it is probably in the storage room or something of that nature. And that data, from the point that it is swiped at the keypad to the back of the computer, that is where it is vulnerable and it is not encrypted. Once it hits that computer and goes through the processing system, that is where it is encrypted and protected.

So what happens is continually we change the standard and these complex, sophisticated criminal actors are going to go after and have been going after this data in whatever they see as the most advantageous, weakest point in the system.

Mr. STUTZMAN. So are you saying that typically, the weakest point is through retailers' entry points? How do they use the retailers' entry points? When I am swiping a card, are they able to follow that data from—

Mr. NOONAN. What they have done is they have actually installed malware into the computer system where it makes the switch from the swipe into the encryption piece, so before it is encrypted they have malware which actually captures the data at that point and exfiltrates the data back out to a different system where the criminal is able to collect it.

Mr. STUTZMAN. Do retailers have the ability to—is there software out there that can prohibit that sort of activity, or what could retailers do to protect that information?

Mr. NOONAN. I am unsure at this point. That would be an industry question to bring up, sir.

Mr. STUTZMAN. All right.

Thank you. I will yield back.

Chairwoman CAPITO. The gentleman yields back.

Mr. Heck?

Mr. HECK. Thank you, Madam Chairwoman.

I would like to begin by asking unanimous consent to enter into the record the letter dated January 10, 2014, from 17 signatories to Chairman Hensarling requesting this hearing. At the same time, I would like to express my public appreciation to you for conducting this hearing.

Chairwoman CAPITO. Thank you. Without objection, it is so ordered.

Mr. HECK. Thank you.

Mr. Noonan, it is a little hard to look at this phenomenon without coming away with an answer to the question of, "Are we winning or losing?" of, "We are losing," at least as measured—not in terms of the number of attacks, but the number of successful attacks and the dollar amount that has successfully been effectively stolen.

So for those of us who aren't especially geeky, among whom I would count myself, can you put this in the simplest terms possible: What is the most important takeaway for those of us sitting here about what it is we can do as Members of Congress to help change that trend line? What is the most important action we could take, policy we could enact, in whatever form, to help?

Mr. NOONAN. It is my belief that if Congress were to assist in coming up with a reporting requirement where if there is a data breach or a company has knowledge of a data breach, that they were to bring that to law enforcement's attention. That is my perspective. That is the Secret Service perspective. Because we are able to, at that point, help with the information-sharing piece that has to go forward to better protect what is going on after the fact.

In other words, it is best for industry to have a point of contact at law enforcement—I make the analogy with a fire: Don't wait until your house is on fire to have the phone number to the fire department.

If industry partners with law enforcement and already has a personal, a trusted relationship with law enforcement, we, law enforcement, are better able to assist a victim company walk through the process. And in doing so, we are able to grab and gather the cybersecurity-related information and share that, then, with the greater infrastructure in an effort to prevent other attacks.

We use, again, a number of different efforts to share that information. We use the NCCIC, where they are able to push it out through their sources to greater industry. We are able to use our electronic crimes task forces. We are able to push that out to our trusted partners in the private sector as well as academia. And we are able to use our partners at the FS-ISAC to be able to take that information and push it.

So I think the important part of this whole mechanism that we are talking about is the information-sharing apparatus of when a breach does occur, what can we learn from that breach, and how can we share that information to prevent others?

Mr. HECK. I want to ask a follow-up corollary to that, which is really a follow up to the question—he has left now—Mr. Luetkemeyer asked, which I didn't think you answered; I didn't think you were evading it but I didn't think you actually answered it, and I really thought it was a very good question, especially given that the nature of this activity does not respect boundaries of countries whatsoever. He asked you, "What could we do to help you be more effective internationally?"

And basically what you said is, "Well, these international partnerships are really important to us."

But the question, sir, is, what can we do to help you be more effective as it relates to your ability to engage in effective enforcement internationally?

Mr. NOONAN. You can continue to support the Secret Service in our efforts of continuing to expand our presence in our international field offices and expanding that footprint. You can help us in furthering our international working groups that we have. We have working groups in the Ukraine; we have international working groups—

Mr. HECK. Just use one example.

Mr. NOONAN. I'm sorry.

Mr. HECK. I got it. I have one other question that I want to ask, and I apologize—

Mr. NOONAN. Sure. No problem.

Mr. HECK. —for interrupting. I want to go back to Target.

It is my understanding that neither Target-branded debit cards or credit cards were breached, or successfully—and first of all, I would like to know if I have accurate information in that regard. And if it is true, what was the difference? And is there a lesson to be learned there if it is true? What were they doing such that information wasn't used against—

Mr. NOONAN. Sure. So, I just checked, and that information is not accurate. Those cards—

Mr. HECK. They were breached.

Mr. NOONAN. —were breached as well, so that was taken.

Mr. HECK. Thank you.

Mr. NOONAN. Yes, sir.

Mr. HECK. I yield back the balance of my entire 6 seconds. Thank you, Madam Chairwoman.

Chairwoman CAPITO. The gentleman yields back.

Mr. McHenry?

Mr. MCHENRY. I thank the chairwoman.

I just have a broad question for both of you, and if you could answer this. I read news reports that merchants and universities are finding out about data breaches from the government, from financial institutions, from credit card companies, banks, the whole lot. Why are merchants failing to detect those security breaches?

Mr. NOONAN. I can't answer why they are not detecting the security breaches, but law enforcement as well as other parts of the private sector—banks, processing companies—have a unique perspective of looking at compromised data. So we can be working with bank investigators—you can take any bank for example—and when they start seeing different anomalies with their customer base of reporting fraud losses, the initial point of report is going to be back to the bank investigator or back to the bank.

So when they start seeing high percentages of fraud loss coming from the same merchant or the same retailer, that is a concern, so they would either bring it to law enforcement's attention or actually bring it to the retailer's attention at that point. So not necessarily would the retailer have the exposure themselves of that—

Mr. MCHENRY. Okay. But to that end, Mr. Noonan, when you announced the data breach with Visa and Target in August of 2013, right, it was made public then. Am I right on the timeline?

Mr. NOONAN. Negative. On Target? It wasn't until December at some point.

Mr. MCHENRY. Okay. So when did you all identify the malware for that data breach?

Mr. NOONAN. The data breach, when it was brought to—when we were working closely side by side with the forensic examiners that—the third-party forensic examiners that Target had hired, within a week we were able to have that data and be able to push that out to—

Mr. MCHENRY. So, you turned it around in a week's time?

Mr. NOONAN. Yes, sir.

Mr. MCHENRY. Okay. So on the next panel, we have a witness from the Financial Services Information and Sharing and Analysis Center, and they are going to—they are actually conducting a study which, "engages machine-to-machine threat intelligence exchange in a way that will more quickly inform financial infrastructure front line operators and aid their preventative and incident response decision-making." They are calling this the Cyber Threat Intelligence Repository.

Are you both familiar with this initiative?

Mr. ZELVIN. We are, sir. At the NCCIC, we are one of the leading proponents and creators of the STIX and TAXII framework to which you are referring.

Mr. MCHENRY. So will this speed the response? Tell us the value of it.

Mr. ZELVIN. Sure, Congressman. I think one of the best ways to highlight this is in September 2012, our financial sector was being attacked about 3 times a week with something called "distributed denial of service attacks." We were getting information by the hundreds of thousands, and technical information. We were getting those—and I am going to use some generalisms just to illustrate the point—in PDFs, so, in a very user-unfriendly format for a cybersecurity defender.

We started using spreadsheets like Excel, which was a little bit better, but there are a variety of different data formats that companies use so there wasn't a one-size-fits-all. The STIX and TAXII format will enable to us adjust the information so somebody doesn't have to e-mail it, we don't have to process it, we then e-mail it back. This will do it in an automatic way so what had been taking us days that we got down into hours will hopefully take us seconds.

Mr. McHenry. So you move from PDFs to Excel—

Mr. Zelvin. To a machine-to-machine format that will take the human out of the equation. Again, it will be up to the—where the destination goes how they are going to want to process—

Mr. McHenry. My time is short, but can you tell us the legal restrictions that prohibit greater data-sharing? What are the things we could do to make the dissemination of data better?

Mr. Zelvin. Congressman, I am going to highlight something that is—the question that was asked of Mr. Noonan, and you may have asked it. One of the things that we would really ask Congress to do is just better define clarity on information-sharing. What is information that the private sector and others can share with us?

I will tell you, we meet with a lot of C-suite executives, the security folks, and they say, ''By all means, government, here, you can have this information. Proliferate it widely. Others are being attacked. This will help us all.''

Then they have others in the company who are giving good advice—their lawyers—saying, ''Look, there is no legal means that allows this. We are assuming some risk, some liability here.'' If we could get some clarity as to what can be shared with us and have that in law, that will really speed the process. And also, it should be respectful of privacy and civil liberties.

We should not do this without having some governance on us, but it should not stop us from doing it, either.

Mr. McHenry. I thank the chairwoman for her advocacy on this important issue.

Chairwoman Capito. Mr. Rothfus?

Mr. Rothfus. Thank you, Madam Chairwoman.

In Pittsburgh, we are fortunate to have premier academic institutions like Carnegie Mellon University and the University of Pittsburgh right at our doorsteps. Both of these universities are doing exceptional work in the area of data security.

And, Mr. Noonan, you highlighted in your testimony the work of Carnegie Mellon.

As you, I think, would both agree, we need to be using these great resources in our fight to combat data-breachers.

I am wondering, Mr. Noonan, if you would elaborate a little bit on how the Secret Service—and then, Mr. Zelvin, if you could perhaps comment on what DHS has been doing with these and similarly situated universities around the country?

Mr. Noonan. Yes, sir. Thank you.

The University Carnegie Mellon, we work closely with their Software Engineering Institute. We actually have a full-time agent who is assigned there, so he is sitting at Carnegie Mellon, partnered with them. Through academia and observing what is occurring in a lot of these cyber incidents, we are able to develop other tools—technical tools—which the Software Engineering Institute is able to help us identify different situations, different forensic solutions, different ways of looking at data, which better helps us do our cases, our investigations, our information-sharing.

Like the institution at Carnegie Mellon, we also have representation at the University of Tulsa, where we have the Cell Phone or

Mobile Device Forensics Facility, which we worked closely with students—graduate student level students there—and we look at how mobile devices can be affected by criminals. We take highly complex criminal cases and we push them to our agent who sits with the University of Tulsa to examine how to get at those forensic capabilities and those forensic hurdles in mobile devices, too.

So it is very important for us to team with academia to decide what is on the horizon of the next threat.

Mr. ROTHFUS. Mr. Zelvin, is DHS similarly engaged with the academic institutions?

Mr. ZELVIN. Congressman, we are. Carnegie Mellon is one of our most critical partners in not only understanding threats but also in the mitigation, so it is an intimate relationship and something that we hold in the highest regard.

Mr. ROTHFUS. I want to follow up a little bit on what Representative McHenry was talking about. I think everyone can agree that effective data security is dependent on a voluntary collaboration between the government and members of the private sector. Key to establishing this sort of trust-based public-private partnership is adequate legal liability protection for private entities that share information with the government.

And to that end, could you please elaborate on the current policy regarding legal liability protection for private entities that opt to share threat information with agencies like yours? Maybe each of you can—

Mr. ZELVIN. Congressman, that is one of the central issues with sharing at government is the concern of either breaking the law or potentially having court action in a civil case. So, there is great desire on behalf of the Executive Branch to have the legal liabilities in place so one would not be punished for sharing with government. Again, the information should be clarified as to what can be shared, but if you do share that information, one should be able to do so without penalty.

Mr. ROTHFUS. Mr. Noonan, can you comment on, from your perspective, the current policy with respect to information-sharing?

Mr. NOONAN. Yes, sir. I don't believe there is a policy as of right now. So I would concur with Mr. Zelvin. I think there is an issue with companies coming forward so they are given some sort of protection, but I cannot comment on existing policy, sir, no.

Mr. ROTHFUS. In both of your written testimonies, you discuss the increasingly international nature of the threat landscape and the need for close partnerships with foreign law enforcement agencies. Which countries are you most concerned about in terms of data security?

Mr. NOONAN. A number of the international cases that we are talking about today are Eastern European, Russian-speaking cyber criminals. I don't want to affiliate these type of criminals with one particular country because again, there are no borders.

We see Eastern European, Russian-speaking cyber criminals who are here domestically in our country that we are able to arrest and bring to justice. We see these types of criminals all over the world.

I say this in the fact that these are the most sophisticated, in our opinion, cyber criminals who are attacking our Nation's financial infrastructure. So as far as saying—in trying to lock it down to a particular country of origin, there is not one in particular. We are seeing them across-the-board.

But again, the Russian-speaking cyber criminal is using the Russian language as a form of OPSEC, if you will, to provide some anonymity to them. Because they use the Internet, they are wallowing in the anonymity of the Internet.

Mr. ROTHFUS. Mr. Zelvin, would you agree with the Russian-speaking actors out there? Are there other countries about which you have particular concerns?

Mr. ZELVIN. Congressman, I worry about actors in Asia; I worry about actors in Europe, to include Eastern Europe. It is literally a global threat environment. So on the financial side, I would agree with Mr. Noonan, it is more the Eastern European criminal actors, but there is also extraordinary criminal activity in Asia, as well.

Mr. ROTHFUS. Thank you.

And thank you, Madam Chairwoman.

Chairwoman CAPITO. Thank you.

Mr. Barr?

Mr. BARR. Thank you, Madam Chairwoman.

I wanted to kind of know from the witnesses what the worst-case scenario would be. In your all's professional judgment, what would be the greatest cybersecurity threat to America's financial system?

Mr. NOONAN. In my opinion, it is a financial services attack that goes unnoticed. So a long, long period of exposure to a financial services sector company is my opinion of what the worst case could be.

It is through the actions of law enforcement that proactively go out and seek these out that brings it to industry's attention. And I also think it is important that when industry itself notices it, that they bring it to our attention.

It is important for us—law enforcement, the government—to be able to either prevent the attack from happening or see it as it is happening to be able to stop the bleeding from happening. If the bleeding occurs for a long, long period of time and there is a long period of exposure, that, in the financial services sector, would be probably the more important, more area of concern for that sector.

Mr. BARR. Mr. Noonan, what would prevent a victim or targeted company from failing to notice this attack?

Mr. NOONAN. In my opinion, it is how advanced these criminal actors are. So when we are talking about significant criminal actors that—you have to understand, when they are going after the financial services sector, they are going into these targeted victim companies stealthily. Their job is to go undetected, because if they are detected and they go into these situations loud and disrupt everything, they are going to lose what their goal is and that is their financial gain; that is their grabbing the data and being able to monetize that data.

So if law enforcement and industry learns about the theft of that data and we are able to do something about it, it minimizes the criminal profit in what they are attempting to do.

Mr. BARR. Have we been able to assess or gauge the capabilities of some of these hackers? Specifically, the kind of nightmare scenario would be something along the lines of a hacker being able to erase electronic data from a large financial institution, or worse, effectuate transactions through hacking into a large, systemically important financial institution.

Are we aware of whether or not cyber terrorists have that capability at this point?

Mr. ZELVIN. Congressman, let me answer that and then maybe go back to your original question. There are actors out there who have extraordinary sophistication, who are patient and are looking for vulnerabilities and are absolutely capable of finding them quickly, and it is just whether or not they have the intent and the access and then the ability.

As I look at the worst-case scenario, to answer the first part of your question, I think that if somebody was to find an intrusion in the transactional systems that the financial sector uses, that would be pretty catastrophic. If there is a loss of confidence within the systems themselves where data has been compromised, that would be pretty catastrophic. If consumers lose the convenience that they rely upon, are unable to use their credit cards and their ATMs, that would be pretty catastrophic.

There are others but those are the three that really come to my mind. You really get to that high impact, low probability.

The sector, the institutions are doing extraordinary work at this every hour of every day. But ultimately, there are vulnerabilities and the actors are using some very creative and clever means to come at us, so you have to be very good every single day because they are trying to come at you every single minute of every day.

Mr. BARR. And in terms of technological advancements in terms of creating defenses to this, there is talk about these chip cards and more extensive use of PINs, particularly with credit cards. But I did notice that in the case of the Target situation, that PINs were procured by the hackers, as well. So how effective is expanded use of PINS as a defense mechanism?

Mr. NOONAN. Any added security measure is going to definitely help in the monetization of whatever data is stolen. It would not assist in the theft of the data itself.

Mr. BARR. Right.

Mr. NOONAN. Chip and PIN technology will help in limiting the criminal monetization of that data, but it would not help in the theft of that data. That data could still be used on card-not-present purchases.

So a cyber criminal, though he cannot re-encode that data onto a credit card and use that counterfeit credit card, he could go online and type in the 16-digit number and the other information that is exposed there and still accomplish financial loss to the victim bank or the victim institution.

Mr. BARR. Thank you.

I yield back the balance of my time.

Chairwoman CAPITO. Thank you.

The gentleman yields back, and that concludes questioning for the first panel.

I want to thank both of you gentlemen. I think this has been very enlightening, and I again apologize for the delay and thank you for your patience. You are dismissed.

While we are changing over, I am going to ask for unanimous consent to submit several statements for the record from the Independent Community Bankers of America; the National Retail Federation; the National Association of Federal Credit Unions; the American Bankers Association; and the Credit Union National Association.

Without objection, it is so ordered.

All right. I want to thank the second panel for coming in. We have a second panel of distinguished witnesses.

Again, thank you for your patience. I know you have been sitting here, as well, while we had our technical difficulties.

Each of you will be recognized for 5 minutes to give an oral presentation of your testimony. And without objection, each of your written statements will be made a part of the record.

Our first witness is Mr. Troy Leach, chief technology officer, PCI Security Standards Council.

Welcome, Mr. Leach.

STATEMENT OF TROY LEACH, CHIEF TECHNOLOGY OFFICER, PAYMENT CARD INDUSTRY (PCI) SECURITY STANDARDS COUNCIL (SSC)

Mr. LEACH. Thank you.

My name is Troy Leach, and I am the chief technology officer for the PCI Security Standards Council, a global industry initiative that is focused on security payment card data. Our approach to an effective security program is people, process, and technology as key parts of data protection. Our community of over 1,000 of the world's leading businesses tackles security challenges from simple issues—for example, the word "password" is still one of the most commonly used passwords—to very complex issues, like proper encryption key management.

We understand when consumers are upset when their payment card data is put at risk and the harm that is caused by breaches. The Council was created as a forum for all stakeholders—banks, merchants, manufacturers, and others—to proactively protect consumers' cardholder data against emerging threats.

Our standards focus on removing cardholder data if it is no longer needed. Our mantra is simple: If you don't need it, don't store it. If you do need it, then protect it through a multilayered approach and devalue it through innovative technologies that reduce incentives for criminals to steal it.

Let me explain how we do that. The data security standard is built on 12 principles that cover everything from strong access control, monitoring and testing of networks, risk assessment, and much more. This standard is updated regularly through feedback from our global community.

In addition, we have developed other standards that cover payment software, security manufacturing of cards, point-of-sale devices, and much more. We also develop standards and guidance on emerging technologies, like tokenization and point-to-point encryption, that remove the amount of card data that is kept in systems, rendering it useless to cyber criminals.

Another technology, EMV chip, has widespread use in Europe and other markets and is an extremely effective method of reducing card fraud in face-to-face environments. That is why the Council supports the deployment of this technology. In fact, today we already certified a securing of chip terminals and manufacturing of chip cards.

However, EMV chip is only one piece of the puzzle. In addition, controls are needed to protect the integrity of payments online, on the telephone, and in other channels. These controls include encryption, proper access, response from tampering, malware protection, and more.

These are all addressed within the PCI standards today. Used together, EMV chip and PCI standards can provide strong protections for payment card data.

But effective security requires more than just standards and technology. Without ongoing adherence and supporting programs, these are only tools and not solutions.

The Council makes it easy for businesses to choose products that have been independently lab-tested and certified as secure. The Council's certification and training programs have educated tens of thousands of individuals including assessors, merchants, technology companies, and government. And finally, we conduct global campaigns to raise awareness of payment card security.

The recent compromises demonstrate the importance of a multilayered approach to payment card security, and there are clear ways in which the government can help—for example, by leading stronger law enforcement efforts worldwide, particularly because of the global nature of these threats; and by encouraging stiff penalties for these crimes. Promoting information-sharing between the public and private sector also merits attention.

The Council is an active collaborator with government. We work with NIST, DHS, and many other government entities, and we are ready and willing to do more. We believe that the development of standards to protect payment card data is something that we are uniquely qualified to do. The global reach, expertise, and flexibility of PCI have made it an extremely effective mechanism for protecting consumers if implemented correctly.

The recent breaches underscore the complex nature of payment card security. A multifaceted problem cannot be solved by a single technology, mandate, or regulation. It cannot be solved by a single sector of society.

Businesses, standards bodies, policymakers, and law enforcement must work together to protect the financial and privacy interests of consumers.

Today, as this committee focuses on recent breaches, we know that criminals are focusing on inventing the next attack. There is no time to waste. The PCI Council and business must continue to provide multilayered security protections while Congress leads efforts to combat global cyber crimes that threaten us all.

We thank the committee for its attention to this, and we look forward to finding a way forward with addressing large security concerns of our time.

[The prepared statement of Mr. Leach can be found on page 67 of the appendix.]

Chairwoman CAPITO. Thank you.

Our next witness is Mr. Greg Garcia, advisor, Financial Services Information Sharing and Analysis Center.

Welcome.

STATEMENT OF GREGORY T. GARCIA, ADVISOR, FINANCIAL SERVICES INFORMATION SHARING AND ANALYSIS CENTER (FS–ISAC)

Mr. GARCIA. Thank you, Chairwoman Capito, Ranking Member Meeks, and members of the subcommittee.

I am Greg Garcia, president of Garcia Cyber Partners, a cybersecurity policy and business development consulting firm. I am testifying here today as an advisor to the Financial Services Information Sharing and Analysis Center, or FS-ISAC.

In light of the recent data breaches in the retail sector, this hearing is timely as we consider how commercial and critical infrastructure sectors can prevent and defend against such attacks from happening in the future.

During my tenure as Assistant Secretary at Homeland Security and as an executive with the financial services sector and IT sectors, I have consistently held up the FS-ISAC as a model operation. It is a model for how trusted collaboration, timely intelligence, and information-sharing are essential elements of any risk management strategy. They are effective tools against cyber adversaries who would subvert the integrity of the critical infrastructures that maintain the cyber, physical, and economic security of this country and the world.

So accordingly, I would like to spend just the next few minutes describing some of the major elements of the model and put it in the context of the recent data breaches that are the subject of this hearing.

The FS-ISAC was founded in 1999 in acknowledgement of a Presidential Directive, PDD 63, which urged private industry to self-organize around the mission of sector-specific critical infrastructure protection. The FS-ISAC provides a formal structure for its 4,500 member institutions to share valuable and actionable cyber intelligence within the sector and with their industry and government partners. This collaborative activity ultimately benefits the Nation.

At FS-ISAC, we use all the tools at our disposal to stay ahead of adversaries. And just a few of these tools include the secure FS-ISAC member Web portal, where threat indicators are published; e-mail listservs; threat assessment conference calls; best practices advisories; incident response and mitigation protocols; cyber exercises; and information-sharing partnerships across the sector, with other sectors, and with government and cyber operations and intelligence entities, such as the NCCIC.

We recognize that the threats we face are sophisticated and are frequently changing, and that immediate sharing of threat details and patterns is effective in heading off the changing nature of the threats.

We also share this sensitive information without the risk that any member company would exploit another's misfortune from cyber attack for competitive advantage. Members know we are all in this together, that an attack on one can very quickly escalate to attack on many if all eyes and ears are not working together.

And our organization ensures that even smaller community institutions have access to threat information alongside the largest financial institutions in the Nation. By way of specific example, allow me to walk you through some of the actions taken by the FS-ISAC in the wake of the retailer data breaches that recently occurred.

First, when information from forensic investigations became available FS-ISAC published a joint document with the DHS National Cybersecurity and Communications Integration Center (NCCIC), the U.S. Secret Service, and ISAC partners regarding the breach. We provided relevant mitigation recommendations and network security best practices from an industry owner and operator perspective. These security practices are intended to help vendors and merchants to secure their point-of-sale systems and to defend against malware that are used in those system attacks.

Second, FS-ISAC encouraged its association members to share the joint document broadly with their members, and we also met with and provided the document to a number of retailer associations and encouraged them to share the document with their members.

Third, as information about the attacks was becoming available, members were able to leverage FS-ISAC's all-hazards playbook and related best practices to better protect and communicate with their customers and the general public.

Fourth, FS-ISAC provided an assessment of the point-of-sale malware to its members on its biweekly threat calls and the assessment examined the malware in several ways—the usage patterns in the short term, the growing popularity and availability of the malware tools, and threat indicators for network defenders.

Finally, we continue to work with multiple associations representing the retailers to explore ways in which we can help them enhance the security of their systems.

Since these data breaches occurred, there has been considerable discussion in the public domain about accountability and assignment of costs associated with these breaches. Indeed, financial institutions have absorbed considerable costs associated with canceling and reissuing credit and debit cards to their customers.

But as I stated at the beginning of my testimony, it is clear to us that we are all in this together, that security is a shared responsibility, and that is why the FS-ISAC was pleased to see the announcement on February 13th of a new partnership between merchant and financial trade associations that will focus on exploring the paths to increased information-sharing, better card security technology, and maintaining the trust of customers. Discussion regarding the partnership was initiated by the Retail Industry Leaders Association and the Financial Services Roundtable and was joined by a dozen other influential financial associations.

Madam Chairwoman, that concludes my testimony and I look forward to answering any questions the subcommittee may have for me.

[The prepared statement of Mr. Garcia can be found on page 57 of the appendix.]

Chairwoman CAPITO. Thank you.

Our next witness is Mr. David Fortney, senior vice president, product manager and development, The Clearing House Payments Company.

Welcome.

STATEMENT OF DAVID FORTNEY, SENIOR VICE PRESIDENT, PRODUCT MANAGEMENT AND DEVELOPMENT, THE CLEARING HOUSE PAYMENTS COMPANY

Mr. FORTNEY. Thank you. Good afternoon, Chairwoman Capito, Ranking Member Meeks, and members of the subcommittee.

My name is David Fortney. I am the senior vice president of product management for The Clearing House, and I thank you for the opportunity to talk today about issues that are critical to all Americans—the security of our payment system and also the protection of sensitive consumer financial information.

The Clearing House is the Nation's oldest bank association and payments company. Our mission includes ensuring the safety, soundness, and efficiency of the payments system.

We provide payment services to our 23 owner banks and other financial institutions, clearing and settling nearly $2 trillion daily. The organization's owner banks collectively represent over half of the Nation's deposits and over 70 percent of Visa and MasterCard-branded credit cards.

The recent escalation of merchant data breaches demonstrates the increasing sophistication of cyber criminals and also underscores the urgent need for financial institutions, merchants, and all who touch the payment system to work together to protect against current and future threats.

I will focus my testimony today on two payment systems technologies that are on the horizon and will reduce the risk of future breaches: EMV; and tokenization.

First, EMV cards contain computer chips and they are designed to protect against counterfeiting, as compared to the magnetic stripe-based cards used today. However, EMV alone would not have prevented the theft of card information in the recent breaches, as it relies on merchants receiving and processing the same static information that account numbers have today. As we have heard from prior testimony, those account numbers would still be significantly valuable to cyber criminals for committing fraud online, where most fraud occurs.

Additionally, as EMV was designed prior to the Internet, prior to mobile phones or tablets, it does not address transactions initiated via those means.

The second technology I would like to discuss is one that we have been directly involved in at The Clearing House. It is called tokenization.

Tokenization addresses online and mobile phone payments by substituting a limited-use random number, called a digital token, for the customer's account number during the transaction. Working behind the scenes, the secure digital token acts just like a regular account number as it goes through the system and requires very little change in how customers and merchants operate. A customer's true account number is never present in the smartphone or in the merchant's system, preventing any malware residing on those systems from capturing that sensitive information in the first place.

The implementation of these two technologies—EMV and tokenization—will require cooperation amongst the banks and merchants as the tangible benefits can only be achieved by moving in tandem.

Turning to e-commerce, today customers provide personal financial and other data to e-commerce merchants, online wallets, alternative payment providers, merchant aggregators, and others. This proliferation of live sensitive customer account data increases the risk of breach-related fraud. When my bank recently sent me a new card after a compromise, I needed to update that card information on 47 different merchant and payment provider Web sites. In a tokenized environment, customer account data is held securely behind the bank firewalls and consumers won't need to update account information when cards are reissued.

The scale of the payment system is enormous, with hundreds of millions of consumers, millions of merchants, thousands of banks and credit unions, and hundreds of networks and processors. The only way to gain broad adoption of a new technology such as tokenization is to develop an open standard that is scalable and widely adopted. Open standards promote innovation and allow customers and merchants to choose the best point-of-sale technology that works best for them.

Two years ago, The Clearing House and its owner banks began working together to create an open tokenization standard that we call Secure Token Exchange. We are working with mobile wallets, networks, merchants, and payment processors to pilot and trial the standard. The initial pilot began late last year and we will soon expand the trial phase to encompass additional banks, merchants, and cities.

This initiative has acted as a catalyst with an increasing number of payment system participants now working on tokenization. We remain very much at the center of this activity.

For example, The Clearing House is now working with the card networks, standard bodies, merchants, and processors on digital tokenization efforts with the goal of upholding the core openness, safety, and soundness principles. We also joined the coalition referred to by the prior witness, a coalition of merchant and financial industry trade associations, to form a cybersecurity partnership.

Thank you again for the opportunity to testify on these critical issues, and I would be happy to answer any questions you may have.

[The prepared statement of Mr. Fortney can be found on page 54 of the appendix.]

Chairwoman CAPITO. Thank you.

Our final witness is Mr. Edmund Mierzwinski, consumer program director, U.S. PIRG.

Welcome.

STATEMENT OF EDMUND MIERZWINSKI, CONSUMER PROGRAM DIRECTOR, U.S. PIRG

Mr. MIERZWINSKI. Thank you, Madam Chairwoman, Ranking Member Meeks, and members of the subcommittee.

As I did at a Senate hearing last month, I want to try to shift the discussion from what it has been in the media anyway, which is simply data breach notification—I am glad today we are talking about a lot more than data breach notification—to many of the other issues surrounding data security.

First, regarding the Target breach, I am very concerned that Target dragged out notification to consumers for a long time. If it was because of investigations conducted with law enforcement that is one thing, but if it is simply because they wanted to drag it out for a long time, I am very disappointed.

I am also disappointed in the product that they gave consumers—credit monitoring lite, a product that only tells you if your Experian credit report has any changes made to it, but not if your other two major credit reports have any changes made on them. Further, in order to accept that product, even though it was free, consumers had to agree to a mandatory arbitration clause limiting their rights against Experian in the future, and that is simply unacceptable to me.

But at the same time, I don't hold Target, Neiman Marcus, or any other company completely to blame for the breaches that have occurred in their stores or in their payment systems. The reason for that is they are working with the banks and the card networks, and the banks and the card networks are forcing them to use an obsolete payment system known as the mag-stripe card. For 50 years, or maybe 40 years, we have used the mag-stripe card without upgrading it.

I am very pleased to hear that the banks are now talking about open standards to upgrade the systems out there. That is very encouraging to me. But for 40 years, they acted as monopolists with closed standards and required merchants to accept a card essentially like a car from the 1950s—no airbags, no ABS brakes, no additional safety features, no safety glass.

Merchants were forced to continue to adopt new and different and ever-changing changes to their systems. It was just very difficult for them and it is not all the merchants' fault, and the banks need to be held accountable and the card networks that were formerly owned by the banks and still are largely controlled by the banks.

I have in my written testimony 10 recommendations that I want to go through quickly.

First, Congress should make all plastic equal. Credit cards are safe by law; debit cards have zero liability by promise only. Plus, with a debit card, again, you are required to use an unsafe system on the signature-based network instead of a PIN-based network.

You are encouraged, anyway, to use it without a PIN, and that is just unfair and unreasonable to consumers who not only are breached, who will not only face the problem of fraud or identity theft, but also lose money from their existing account until the bank replaces it, if it honors the zero liability promise. So first, why shouldn't debit cards have the same consumer protection as credit cards?

Second, be careful not to endorse any specific technologies. Go forward with open standards that push innovation and that all participants in the system are subject to the same rules. Previously, the banks have forced merchants to be subject to a different set of rules than they have been subject to, and companies that are under

Gramm-Leach-Bliley are subject to a different set of rules than the merchants are subject to—an easier, softer set of rules.

Third, look into whether the open standards bodies are truly open. I don't think they have been in the past; I am encouraged to think that they may be in the future.

Fourth, Congress should stay away from an issue that has been debated in State legislatures, which is that banks try to get the merchants, by law, to pay all of their costs. They already do pay most of the banks' costs. It is impossible to do that by law.

Finally, don't preempt the States. Even if you come up with a uniform standard, don't preempt the States. You don't need to. The States will move onto other issues as long as your standard is good enough, but if it isn't, we need the States as first responders.

Make sure you allow for private enforcement by consumers of any law in State attorneys general as well as a good Federal law.

Don't include a harm trigger in your law. Force companies that lost their information to tell us about it.

Investigate overpriced credit monitoring. I have already talked about the fact that it is given for free to consumers, but it is something the committee should investigate and the CFPB has been looking into quite a bit, as well.

Finally, Congress should investigate the over-collection of consumer information generally on the Internet by companies we don't even do business with—not only by our banks, and not only by the retailers with whom we do business. There are dozens if not hundreds of additional business-to-business companies collecting information about us that are not regulated.

Thank you.

[The prepared statement of Mr. Mierzwinski can be found on page 73 of the appendix.]

Chairwoman CAPITO. Thank you very much, and I want to thank all of the witnesses.

I will yield myself 5 minutes to begin the questioning.

My first question is for Mr. Garcia. On the FS-ISAC, it is a sharing organization with the financial services community, are there now private entities who are in that—retailers and such that are a member of that community or is it mostly just financial services?

Mr. GARCIA. It is mostly financial services, although we do have a retailer member now and we include insurance companies, and payment processors. Any organizations that have—that essentially are regulated as financial institutions or have banking credit subsidiaries are eligible for membership in the FS-ISAC.

Chairwoman CAPITO. Would, say, like a Target be eligible for membership to—

Mr. GARCIA. Yes. And they are a member.

Chairwoman CAPITO. And they are a member.

Mr. GARCIA. Yes.

Chairwoman CAPITO. So are you going to encourage other retailers—because obviously this is where the—some of the breaches most recently have taken place—

Mr. GARCIA. Absolutely. We have had a lot of conversations with the retail sector, and certainly Target's membership in the FS-ISAC, I think, serves as leadership and opportunity to bring on the broader retail sector, provided each individual organization is eligible for ISAC membership according to the regulatory status, as I mentioned.

Chairwoman CAPITO. All right. Thank you.

Mr. Fortney, you mentioned two different types of technologies, the EMV chip and the tokenization. Is anybody using the tokenization now in the United States with whom we would all be familiar?

Mr. FORTNEY. Tokenization has been used in what I would call point-to-point or proprietary type of environments, but what is—

Chairwoman CAPITO. Give me an example of that.

Mr. FORTNEY. So, an example would be that instead of using a true account number in a product that maybe one bank issues, instead embed a digital token. That has been done. Or individual merchants—

Chairwoman CAPITO. In financial transactions, not retail.

Mr. FORTNEY. Correct.

Chairwoman CAPITO. Okay.

Mr. FORTNEY. What is new with this is really talking about it in terms of an open standard that could be used widely in which everyone agrees to the same rules—

Chairwoman CAPITO. Is anybody outside the United States using tokenization in a retail spectrum?

Mr. FORTNEY. I believe the United States is ahead in this particular area, although there is a lot of interest for the technology globally, and some—

Chairwoman CAPITO. Okay.

Mr. FORTNEY. For instance, some of the institutions in our owner base do operate globally. They have strong interest in using this technology across the globe.

Chairwoman CAPITO. Okay. The EMV chip is used in Europe, correct?

Mr. FORTNEY. That is correct.

Chairwoman CAPITO. Okay. Now I think I read this or heard that Target—and I am using Target as an example, but it might not be the correct example—had originally looked at the EMV chip as one of the mechanisms that they would use and actually might have even used it at some point and then ceased using it. Is that correct?

Mr. FORTNEY. I read the same thing, and I think it really goes to—it is really impossible for a single entity to introduce a new technology in payment with—and have impact without moving in tandem with a number of other retailers at the same time and the banks at the same time.

Chairwoman CAPITO. Yes. I think in that same article it said that it was discontinued because of the ease of service at the checkout. It was holding people up for one reason or another. Anyway, yes, I was just curious about that.

Mr. Leach, I know from our previous conversation when we talked about the EMV chip, it is not the be-all and end-all to solve these issues. Could you expound on that a little bit for us, please?

Mr. LEACH. Sure. I would be happy to do so.

As you know, our PCI standards are applied in Europe already today, and so we are looking at ways that we can remove the exposure of card data. So in a chip transaction, mag-stripe transaction, the card information is still exposed. And as Mr. Noonan in the previous panel explained, you can take that information and create fraud in online, telephone order, and other channels.

So our focus is on removing that card information completely from the merchant environment through tokenization, point-to-point encryption, and other means, so as soon as the customer puts their information into a point-of-sale terminal, it is removed, and it is no longer available to the criminal if they are able to get into that system.

Chairwoman CAPITO. Okay. We have been talking a lot about cards, and one of the things I mentioned in my opening statement is my interest in mobile payments, and I don't think of those as cards, although they are attached to a card number.

What about security around these? Is that something that is part of what you are looking at for standards, Mr. Leach?

Mr. LEACH. It is. And we think that this new, innovative technology—and there is actually going to be a press release on the framework next week on this—is very exciting. We think that by removing card data, we can actually improve the security of mobile transactions, as well.

Chairwoman CAPITO. Okay. Thank you.

Mr. Meeks?

Mr. MEEKS. Thank you, Madam Chairwoman.

And let me, as a guy who is not tech-savvy at all, say that I appreciate your testimony.

I guess I will start with Mr. Leach. Again, in trying to figure out what we can do as Members of Congress, there is currently no Federal law establishing security standards that merchants and data brokers are required to meet.

My first question is, does this matter? And what is the appropriate role of the Federal Government, in your estimation, in setting a dynamic and effective security standard, and what should the private sector's role be?

And then, in light of the recent breaches at major U.S. retailers, do the existing PCI standards need to be updated?

Mr. LEACH. I will start with the last question, because it is very interesting the timing of these breaches and our most recent update to the standards. Many of the actual incidents that are being reported in the media of how these criminals were able to get into these systems are actually already addressed in our PCI standards today. When these forensic investigations are completed, they typically provide a report of what PCI requirements have failed in those environments in order for a criminal to actually access and steal consumers' cardholder information.

There is enforcement of our standards in the industry today. It is by contract, so it is a financial institution and their contractual relationships with their merchants is how we enforce in our industry today.

For government involvement, I think the FS-ISAC and information-sharing so that we can take what we learn from these investigations and put that into our standards is where we need to have improvement. I think there has actually been in the last couple of years more engagement between the government and the private sector, and we encourage that to go forward.

Mr. MEEKS. Let me ask, I guess, Mr. Mierzwinski: You testified today, as you did before the Senate Banking Committee in early February, where you urged that we should not embrace any specific technology but use and encourage the users to use the highest existing standard to prevent by action of rules of existing players from blocking additional technological improvements and security innovations.

And I am listening, and I am hearing, on one end, and if I get a chance, I will ask Mr. Fortney about tokenization and how that can become a large-scale viable—but could you please elaborate on some of the basic pros and cons of each smart chip card variation, keeping in mind the differences in cost and the susceptibility to fraud, and how any of the resulting fraud losses are divided between merchants and card issuers and consumers?

Mr. MIERZWINSKI. Thank you, Congressman. Again, today is really the first time that I have heard the words "open standards" from the bank and card network industry. They may have talked about it in the past but I have understood the PCI standards body to be totally controlled by the banks and the card networks, and that has been harmful to innovation.

Today, EMV is kind of a standard, but it has different levels of protection, and the card networks would like you to believe that they are moving toward something called "chip and signature," and that is good enough. But chip and signature is designed by them to ride on the old signature-based platform. Anybody can forge a signature.

Chip and PIN is a better solution. Tokenization is also a better solution to part of the problem. Online, using virtual account numbers for each transaction, is another part of the solution.

So I think as long as we are developing standards in a truly open body where you can promote innovation, we are much better off.

Mr. MEEKS. Mr. Fortney, would you alter your answer at all? What is your opinion on the same question?

Mr. FORTNEY. Yes, so, first of all, in the United States, as Mr. Mierzwinski points out, as the chip cards are introduced it is not necessarily going to be mandating a PIN. You can call it chip and choice, that there will be certain transactions that require a PIN just as they do today, such as an ATM machine or certain retailer transactions. Other transactions may be requiring the signature, and certainly underneath a certain dollar amount there may not be either of those.

But regardless of all that, that chip card is fundamentally more secure than the mag-stripe card and is a big advance forward.

Mr. MEEKS. Thank you.

Mr. LUETKEMEYER [presiding]. Thank you.

With that, I will yield myself 5 minutes.

One of the things that is concerning to me is at this point, from what I understand, the banks normally are the ones left holding the bag normally whenever you have one of these breaches, and is there something, Mr. Leach, in the discussion with your group, to find a way to put some liability on the other—the merchant who didn't maybe have the latest technology or didn't exercise the greatest care with his data so that it was breached? Or am I wrong on that? Is there a sharing of liability there?

Mr. LEACH. The PCI Council is a technical standards body, so liability and all of the enforcement of our standards is managed through those banking relationships between the bank and the merchant. What we do is we try to remove that card information from ever being stored in a merchant location.

We heard from other Congressmen earlier who recognize that security is a very hard thing to do day in and day out, and what we are trying to do, to the gentleman's point earlier about tokenization, is remove cardholder data from ever being exposed in merchant locations so there is no longer an ability for criminals to monetize that data.

Mr. LUETKEMEYER. Mr. Garcia, is there a movement to have higher standards for the merchants so that they share some of the liability there?

Mr. GARCIA. We discussed just this recent partnership consortium that has been established between the financial services sector and merchants and payment processors, and I think that is going to go a long way to sort of gaining a common understanding as to what are our respective vulnerabilities, our respective responsibilities, and how do we work together to stay ahead of the adversaries.

Mr. LUETKEMEYER. Okay. You made mention a while ago that there was a February agreement to that effect. Is that correct?

Mr. GARCIA. That is correct, February 13th.

Mr. LUETKEMEYER. Can you explain that just a little bit further?

Mr. GARCIA. There are about a dozen industry associations that are signatory to this. It is just in the beginning phases. It is a partnership that is based on the recognition that we all—this is a shared challenge and therefore a shared responsibility, and over the coming months we are going to be looking into what are the various initiatives and programs we can engage in together to think about not just new technological capabilities, but what are standards of practice? How do we interact among each other to have a more secure ecosystem for the commercial and retail financial environments?

Mr. LUETKEMEYER. Okay. Do you work with foreign countries, as well, foreign clearinghouses?

Mr. GARCIA. No, not that I am aware of at this point. It is U.S.-based.

Mr. LUETKEMEYER. Okay. With your chip technology changing—or perhaps changing—where do you go with that when it comes to discussing it with merchants who—for instance, if I want to take a trip to Italy and now I want to use my credit card, how is that going to work if they don't have that same technology to be able to accept that card?

This is going to have to be worldwide, I assume. Either Mr. Garcia or Mr. Fortney here?

Mr. FORTNEY. You have hit upon an issue that has been out there for people who travel from country to country, and maybe the card technology they work in one country doesn't work fully in the other. There are a number of banks today that will issue cards that will work internationally, using EMV, and as the rest of the U.S. industry issues those cards over the next year or two, that problem should diminish greatly.

Mr. LUETKEMEYER. One of the problems that we have is with convenience comes more exposure, more risk, and that means more responsibility on an individual's part, too. Is there something an individual can do to protect his cards, his information better by the way he uses it?

Mr. Fortney?

Mr. FORTNEY. You are asking an interesting question because I don't really put a lot of the responsibility on the end user. The end user, when they are in a payments environment, they need to enter their card information in the way in order to get the purchase done. So I guess I would prefer to focus on what are ways that we can actually improve the system, get rid of these card numbers and live static information out of the system and protect the consumers in that way?

Now, to further answer your question, sure there are some things that we all would agree are very bad practices, like if you have a PIN, don't write it on the back of your card, and if you are missing a card or you see a fraudulent transaction, report it promptly. I would encourage people to sign up for the mobile banking alerts that most financial institutions offer so that you have rapid information if your card has been used, and if you don't recognize that transaction, take quick action.

Mr. LUETKEMEYER. Does a consumer need to change his cards regularly? In other words, if I have a MasterCard, for instance, do I need to call the company and say, once every 6 months get a new card with new numbers and—is that a protection or is that just a waste of my time?

Mr. FORTNEY. I don't think that is really necessary because if your card number were to be breached then your institution would most likely reissue that card. This really would be a tremendous hassle for a consumer to proactively go about asking for a new card.

If you have reason to believe it has been breached, absolutely, but not just as a preventative measure. I wouldn't recommend that.

Mr. LUETKEMEYER. My wife, this past couple of weeks, has been in a different State, and as a result, she has used her credit card, and because it was a different State, immediately the credit card company, zam, they said, "Hey, your card is being used in a different State. Is this what you want to—are you there or did somebody steal your card?" It was very quick because the first transaction she did, immediately it was like that, the thing popped up on our e-mail and I was immediately notified to that effect.

It was very helpful and it is nice to know that they are that quick to respond. So I guess that is another way that the companies are trying to prevent some folks from being abused with regards to that.

Mr. FORTNEY. Yes, that is correct. And as you saw in your personal experience, many of the banks—really all of the banks now have this kind of fraud detection technology and they are looking for anything that is outside of the pattern.

That can certainly create a hassle if you are traveling and it happens to you erroneously, but typically you can call and get that—verify the last transaction and the card gets opened up again for a full purchase.

Mr. LUETKEMEYER. Very good. Thank you.

With that, we will move to the gentleman from Georgia, Mr. Scott.

Mr. SCOTT. Thank you very much, Mr. Chairman.

Certainly, first, I just want to commend Mr. Leach and the PCI. I think you guys are on the right track in lessening the available information out there for the bad guys to work with in the first place, and I encourage you to continue with that.

But what really disturbs me about this hearing is that earlier I asked the Secret Service and Homeland Security why the United States was targeted, is there something other nations are doing that we are not doing, and their answer was not an accurate one, if I may say, and I want to address that. Because this is a serious problem and there is a reason why we are being targeted, and I want you all to respond to this.

The Economist, in its February 15th article, said that America—this Nation, the United States—leads the world in payment card fraud. It is the only country in which counterfeit card fraud is consistently growing. In fact, the United States currently accounts for nearly half—47 percent—of all global payment card losses.

It goes on to say, in part, that fraudsters target the United States because that is where the cards are. At the end of 2013 there were 1.2 billion debit, credit, and prepaid cards in circulation in America. That is over half of the 2 billion—more than in any other region. That is nearly five cards per adult here.

But America also makes things easy for fraudsters. Alone among developed countries, it still relies exclusively on cards with magnetic strips, which are far less secure than the chip and PIN technology used elsewhere. So clearly, the gentlemen with Homeland Security and the Secret Service are probably not aware of this.

But now that we are aware of this, Mr. Mierzwinski, let me ask you, given this information from The Economist, given how big this issue is, let me ask you: What makes the United States payment card so vulnerable to fraud more than any other nation, and what is it that we do differently than other countries around the world regarding this?

Mr. MIERZWINSKI. Mr. Scott, I think you answered the question already. I don't know how much I can add to it, but we are still using a 40- or 50-year-old magnetic stripe obsolete technology. We are now starting to move slowly toward chip and PIN, tokenization, virtual card numbers on the Internet, and other solutions that are going to be better.

But the second thing that we do in this country is we aggressively rolled out debit cards to be used without PINs. When they were exclusively ATM cards they required a PIN, but the big card networks wanted them to ride along on their signature-based systems and so they said, "Merchants and consumers, use the unsafe product on the signature-based system."

So that is why we say, let's give consumers greater consumer protection when they use debit cards. And let's go back to encouraging the use of PIN-based networks. There are competitor PIN-based networks but the big banks don't want you to use them because they don't own them.

Mr. SCOTT. I see.

Let me ask you this, because I am anxious—and all of us on this committee are anxious—to see what we in Congress can do. So let me ask you, is there any reason why Congress shouldn't mandate that payment card security standards use the most effective technology in the marketplace?

Mr. MIERZWINSKI. I agree with you on that completely, and I will leave it up to your legislative counsel to help draft it, but absolutely it should be a standard-based system that promotes the highest and most innovative standards.

Mr. SCOTT. And so don't you feel—let me just ask you this: Why is it important, in your opinion—and others can comment on this as well—for Congress to improve debit ATM card consumer rights and make all plastic equal?

Mr. MIERZWINSKI. Very simply, cards are not protected and your bank account is not protected, and that is a real problem for consumers. I believe that if the consumer rights were increased to the level of credit cards—I only use credit cards, by the way, on the Internet, and I only use credits cards at the store. It is the safer way to go. But if debit cards had higher consumer rights that would focus the mind of the banks on improving protections for those cards.

Mr. SCOTT. And you also mentioned that if fraud victims are reimbursed at what you refer to as zero liability, is this zero liability policy ubiquitous among all credit card and debit card users?

Mr. MIERZWINSKI. As far as I—zero liability is something that the debit card industry promotes. The credit card law maximizes our liability at $50, but with a debit card, you could lose all the money in your account under some circumstances.

Mr. SCOTT. Okay. My—

Mr. MIERZWINSKI. But as far as I know, all the card companies do use zero liability but some have more asterisks, more exceptions.

Mr. SCOTT. And so my final point is, because I think the American people—I think this is a problem of soaring magnitude, and we are going to be in trouble if we don't get a handle on this. We in Congress, there is no national directive here, so I just want to ask each of you, do you feel that the most important thing we can do right now is this national breach legislation that we have been talking about, that we have a national standard, or do you see just leaving it at the State level—the various State levels, this hodgepodge that we have?

Mr. MIERZWINSKI. If you are starting with me, I have already testified that I think that we don't really need a national standard, but if you do establish one—because a good, smart company can just comply with the strongest State law, but if we are going to focus on that as part of the solution, just don't preempt the States. Go to a high, good national standard. You won't need to preempt the States.

Mr. SCOTT. Okay.

Anyone else?

Mr. FORTNEY. Yes. We would support a national standard. We just think the most efficient way to deal with these sorts of threats is to be consistent and provide standard consumer protection versus a haphazard, State-by-State approach.

Mr. SCOTT. Yes.

Mr. Garcia?

Mr. GARCIA. Yes. I would agree with that. I think if you have 40-plus State laws that differ in various respects as to what are the requirements for breach notification, it doesn't necessarily improve consumer protection to have multiple different forms of communication, and to the extent that you can standardize that kind of communication to the consumer base nationally, I think that would be more effective and less costly.

Mr. SCOTT. Okay. Thank you.

Mr. Leach, would you—

Mr. LEACH. Consistency is good. Again, we need to find ways to get after these bad guys and remove the monetization of card data, period.

Mr. SCOTT. Okay.

Thank you very much, Mr. Chairman. I appreciate the extra time.

Mr. LUETKEMEYER. Thank you.

I just have one follow-up question here, and then I think we are done for the day and we will let you guys go.

We have seen in the last year or so a number of breaches, and my concern is, how many more are yet to come? And as a result of that, when are we going to get some action taken to stop this?

And so if you could answer those two questions succinctly here, we will start with Mr. Mierzwinski?

Mr. MIERZWINSKI. I apologize—

Mr. LUETKEMEYER. I guess the question is, how susceptible are we to further breaches, and then where are we going to be 5 years from now? Are we going to take action?

Mr. MIERZWINSKI. I think that further breaches are going to occur. I just saw Brian Krebs who is tweeting that—he is the guy who broke the Target story; he is a cyber journalist, I guess—that there was another breach today of a beauty company. And so, there will be continued breaches. The question is, what do we do about them?

Five years from now, I predict we are going to have a much more sophisticated system. There is innovation coming from phone companies, coming from Internet companies, coming from alternatives. It is going to force the banks to do a better job.

Mr. LUETKEMEYER. Mr. Fortney?

Mr. FORTNEY. I would agree with most of that. I think it is not just on the banks, however.

It is really on the banks and the merchants and everyone to work together to introduce these new technologies. It can't be done from one side.

Mr. LUETKEMEYER. Mr. Garcia?

Mr. GARCIA. Asking when we are going to stop cyber attacks is tantamount to asking when we are going to stop crime. It is an ongoing challenge. As long as there is technological innovation, there is technological innovation on the side of criminals as well, finding ways to exploit that.

So, as I mentioned before, it isn't just about technology, but it is about your practices and your information-sharing and your collaboration. We are all in this together and no single one of us is as smart as all of us combined, and that is really what the FS-ISAC is here to talk about today is how we collaborate when those technological solutions aren't going to fully protect us, but what can we do together as a team.

Mr. LUETKEMEYER. I guess the follow-up to you would be, okay, we recognize we have a problem. Your group is one who tries to solve a problem. Are you going to kick it into another gear to get this done ASAP?

Mr. GARCIA. As a matter of fact, we have initiated a new program that tries to automate—that does automate our intelligence and information-sharing and incident response, because as we know, many cyber attacks happen at Internet speed, and as long as we are operating at human speed, we are one step behind. So we have invested quite a lot of resources—FS-ISAC and its membership—in developing—in automated tools using standardized language for how we characterize threats and attacks such that the front-line cyber operators and analysts who are protecting our systems are able to make decisions in a more real-time way and take action in a more real-time way against those threats and attacks.

Mr. LUETKEMEYER. Very good.

Mr. Leach?

Mr. LEACH. I would say we can't address 2014 threats with 2004 controls. We need to remove the legacy systems that we have—and part of that is legacy business process and educating merchants that there is no longer a need to store cardholder information beyond the point of getting an authorization.

I think with the legacy systems that we have today, there is opportunity for us to improve. You asked about what we will see in about 5 years. I see us no longer having these value card information for criminals to attack. That is where I hope we are going to be in 5 years.

Mr. LUETKEMEYER. I thank each of the witnesses for being here today. As you can see, we are very concerned on this side of the table with regards to the privacy of information and the privacy of financial transactions that take place with our consumers and our constituents and the people of this country.

And so, we want to work with you. If you can continue to work with us to point out places where we can be of help, we certainly want to look for that.

And again, I thank the chairwoman for the opportunity to have this hearing.

The Chair notes that some Members may have additional questions for this panel, which they may wish to submit in writing. Without objection, the hearing record will remain open for 5 legislative days for Members to submit written questions to these witnesses and to place their responses in the record. Also, without objection, Members will have 5 legislative days to submit extraneous materials to the Chair for inclusion in the record.

With that, hearing is adjourned.

[Whereupon, at 1:09 p.m., the hearing was adjourned.]

APPENDIX

March 5, 2014

CMW Opening Statement
Financial Institutions Subcommittee Hearing entitled "Data Security: Examining Efforts to Protect Americans' Financial Information"
Wednesday, March 5, 2014
Room 2128, 10:00 AM

Thank you, Chair Capito for scheduling this hearing on the important topic of how we can better safeguard the sensitive financial information of consumers.

The recent high-profile data breaches have raised pressing concerns about the safety and security of critical consumer information – such as credit and debit card accounts and other personally identifiable information.

This is an issue that is not going away.

Testimony from the Secret Service makes it clear that the recent attacks on large retailers are just the latest in a string of breaches.

They recognize that there has been, quote, a "*marked increase in the quality, quantity, and complexity of cyber crimes targeting private industry,*" and that the data breaches of Target and Neiman Marcus are, quote, "*just the most recent, well-publicized examples of this decade-long trend of major data breaches perpetrated by cyber criminals who are intent on targeting our Nation's retailers and financial payment systems.*"

It's troubling to me that despite the increasing prevalence and scale of these attacks, we don't seem to be much closer to protecting consumer's credit and debit account information.

Instead of using this committee to attack the data collection and security procedures of government watchdogs like the highly successful Consumer Financial Protection Bureau, we should be exploring how we can take action to better protect against these types of massive security lapses in a bipartisan manner.

Despite extensive efforts to share information among industry, law enforcement and other stakeholders, a surprising number of breaches go undetected for far too long. A 2013 Data Breach Investigation report conducted by Verizon, found that 66 percent of breaches took "months or more" to be discovered. This is unacceptable and must change.

Clearly, law enforcement, regulators and businesses tasked with safeguarding consumer's information must do more to identify when and where breaches occur – and notify consumers about it as quickly as possible.

Finally, although they are not here today, the CFPB and the FTC should be applauded for their work to equip consumers with the information they need to protect themselves in the event they fall victim. I hope to learn more today about what action industry and government can proactively take to better protect consumers' data.

I look forward to the witnesses' testimony and yield back.

Testimony of David Fortney
The Clearing House Payments Company
House Committee on Financial Services
Subcommittee on Financial Institutions and Consumer Credit
March 5, 2014

Good morning Chairman Capito, Ranking Member Meeks, and members of the subcommittee. My name is David Fortney, Senior Vice President of Product Development and Management for The Clearing House Payments Company. Thank you for the opportunity to talk about issues critical to all Americans – the security of our payments system and the protection of sensitive consumer financial information.

The Clearing House is the nation's oldest banking association and payments company, founded in 1853. Our mission is to ensure the safety, soundness and efficiency of the payments system in particular, and to enhance financial stability more generally. As such, we provide payment, clearing, and settlement services to our twenty-three owner banks and other financial institutions, clearing and settling nearly $2 trillion daily. The Clearing House also engages in cutting-edge thought leadership on payments technology and payments system security. The organization's owner banks collectively represent over 55% of the nation's deposits; over 40% of debit cards; and over 70% of Visa and MasterCard-branded credit cards.

The recent escalation of merchant data breaches demonstrates the increasing sophistication of cybercriminals and underscores the urgent need for financial institutions, merchants, and all who touch the payments system to work together to protect against current and future threats. While banks, along with federal and state laws and regulations, protect consumers against monetary loss, data breaches can result in identity theft and the ensuing consumer impacts of card replacement, account monitoring and fraud reporting, as well as a real loss of confidence in the payments system.

From the other witnesses we have heard about the nature and sophistication of cyber threats, how the recent breaches occurred, and what measures are in place to help prevent future breaches. Like other witnesses, we encourage the adoption of technologies such as point-to-point encryption to ensure that swiped card information is immediately encrypted at the point-of-sale and remains so until it is unlocked behind the firewalls of merchant acquirers.

I will focus the remainder of my testimony on payment system technologies on the horizon that will reduce the risk of future breaches. In particular, two technologies—EMV and tokenization--will play significant roles in protecting against future threats.

EMV, which stands for Europay, MasterCard, and Visa, is a standard for chip-based payments cards and terminals. EMV cards contain embedded integrated circuits and are designed to provide greatly enhanced protection against counterfeiting, as compared to magnetic strip-based cards. As we've heard today, it is relatively easy to produce fake cards with today's magnetic stripe technology.

However, EMV alone would not have prevented the theft of card information in the recent data breaches because it relies on merchants receiving and processing the same static account numbers in use today. Those customer account numbers would still be significantly valuable to cybercriminals for committing fraud online is where most fraud occurs. Additionally, as EMV was designed prior to the Internet, mobile smartphones and tablets, it does not address transactions initiated via those means.

Tokenization addresses online and mobile phone payments by substituting a limited-use random number—a digital token—for the customer's account number during the transaction. Working behind the scenes, the secure digital token acts just like a regular account number as it goes through the system and requires very little change in how customers and merchants operate. The digital token is refreshed regularly, as often as after each purchase. A customer's true account number is never present in the smartphone or in the merchant's system, preventing malware residing on these systems from capturing that information in the first place. Even if the system is compromised, the digital token is of limited or no use to criminals. The customer's real account number remains securely stored in bank data vaults residing behind firewalls at highly-regulated and closely-examined financial institutions or payments networks.

The implementation of these two technologies—EMV and tokenization—will require cooperation amongst banks and merchants as the tangible benefits can only be achieved by moving in tandem. The timeline for the move to EMV in the U.S. has been established by the card networks, and we are pleased to see the recent statements by merchants and financial institutions announcing the acceleration of their individual EMV adoption timelines. As mobile smartphones and other smart devices such as smart watches become increasingly prevalent and enabled for commerce, there is little doubt that payments will increasingly be initiated by these devices in the future. While tokenization is a much newer technology, we are working to see it rapidly standardized and adopted to provide needed protection against future cyberattacks.

Today, customers provide personal financial data to merchants, online wallets, alternative payments providers, merchant aggregators, and others. This proliferation of "live" sensitive customer account data increases the risk of breach-related fraud and presents a confusing and complicated process for consumers to maintain. When my bank sent me a new card last year after a data breach, I needed to update the card information on 47 different merchant and payment provider websites. In a tokenized environment, customer account data is held securely behind bank firewalls, and consumers won't need to update account information when cards are reissued.

Tokenization mitigates the risk of sensitive data being compromised, greatly benefiting both consumers and merchants. Tokenization can be implemented in back-end processing systems with banks and payment processors being the ones responsible for deployment. Merchants will no longer need to keep and safeguard vast quantities of sensitive data. They will still be able to track customer purchases for performing analyses and driving targeted offers, and customers will enjoy a much more secure payments system.

With hundreds of millions of consumers, millions of merchants, thousands of banks and credit unions and hundreds of networks and processors, the only way to gain broad adoption of tokenization and ensure a consistent customer experience is to develop an open tokenization standard. Open standards promote innovation and allow customers and merchants to choose the point-of-sale technology that works best for them. But it will require banks, merchants, networks and processors to work together to accomplish these goals.

Two years ago, The Clearing House and its owner banks began working together to create an open tokenization standard called Secure Token Exchange. We are working with mobile wallets, networks, merchants and payments processors to pilot and trial the standard. The initial pilot began late last year, and we will soon expand the trial phase to encompass additional banks, merchants and cities. Secure Token Exchange is technology agnostic and focuses on the communications necessary to safely and securely correlate a digital token to a customer's account for transaction processing. By keeping a narrow focus, Secure Token Exchange creates minimal disruption to the current payments ecosystem and promotes innovation throughout. This is especially important at the point-of-sale where customers and merchants should be the ones that choose how they communicate with each other. This initiative has acted as a catalyst, with an increasing number of payments system participants now working on tokenization. We remain very much at the center of this activity.

For example, The Clearing House is now working with the card networks, standards bodies, merchants and processors on digital tokenization efforts with a goal of upholding core openness, and safety and soundness principles. We have also joined a coalition of merchant and financial industry trade associations to form a cybersecurity partnership. We are committed as an organization and a company to protect consumers, merchants, and the entire payments system from cyberattacks.

Thank you again for the opportunity to testify on this critical issue. Everyone involved in the payments ecosystem has a responsibility to work toward the implementation of solutions like point-to-point encryption, EMV and tokenization. Doing so will help ensure that the nation's payments system remains safe, sound, and secure in the decades to come. I am happy to address any questions.

Testimony of

Gregory T. Garcia

On Behalf of the

The Financial Services Information Sharing & Analysis Center

Before the

United States House of Representatives

Financial Institutions and Consumer Credit Subcommittee

March 5, 2014

FS-ISAC BACKGROUND

Chairman Capito, Ranking Member Meeks, and members of the Subcommittee, my name is Gregory T. Garcia. I serve as Advisor to the Financial Services Information Sharing & Analysis Center (FS-ISAC). I want to thank you for this opportunity to address the Financial Institutions and Consumer Credit Subcommittee on the important issue of "Data Security: Examining Efforts to Protect Americans' Financial Information". I appear before you today on behalf of FS-ISAC President Bill Nelson, who is on international travel and regrets his inability to take part in this proceeding.

The FS-ISAC was formed in 1999 in response to the 1998 Presidential Decision Directive 63 (PDD 63), which called for the public and private sectors to work together to address cyber threats to the nation's critical infrastructures. After 9/11, and in response to Homeland Security Presidential Directive 7 (and its 2013 successor, Presidential Policy Directive 21) and the Homeland Security Act, the FS-ISAC expanded its role to encompass physical threats to our sector.

The FS-ISAC is a 501(c)6 nonprofit organization and is funded entirely by its member firms and sponsors. In 2004, there were only 68 members of the FS-ISAC, mostly larger financial services firms. Since that time the membership has expanded to 4,500 organizations including commercial banks and credit unions of all sizes, brokerage firms, insurance companies, payments processors, and 24 trade associations representing virtually all of the U.S. financial services sector.

FS-ISAC PROGRAMS AND OPERATIONS – A MODEL FOR OTHER SECTORS

In light of the recent breach revelations against major retailers, this hearing puts a timely emphasis on the need to consider how commercial and critical infrastructure sectors can prevent such attacks from happening in the future.

Since its founding, the FS-ISAC's operations and culture of trusted collaboration have evolved into what we believe is a successful model for how other industry sectors can organize themselves around this security imperative. The overall objective of the FS-ISAC is to protect the financial services sector against cyber and physical threats and risk. It acts as a trusted third party that provides anonymity to allow members to share threat, vulnerability and incident information in a non-attributable and trusted manner. The FS-ISAC provides a formal structure for valuable and actionable information to be shared amongst members, the sector, and its industry and government partners, which ultimately benefits the nation. FS-ISAC information sharing services and activities include:

- delivery of timely, relevant and actionable cyber and physical email alerts from various sources distributed through the FS-ISAC Security Operations Center (SOC);
- an anonymous online submission capability to facilitate member sharing of threat, vulnerability and incident information in a non-attributable and trusted manner;

- operation of email listservs supporting attributable information exchange by various special interest groups including the Financial Services Sector Coordinating Council (FSSCC), the FS-ISAC Threat Intelligence Committee, threat intelligence sharing open to the membership, the Payment Processors Information Sharing Council (PPISC), the Clearing House and Exchange Forum (CHEF), the Business Resilience Committee, and the Payments Risk Council;
- anonymous surveys that allow members to request information regarding security best practices at other organizations;
- bi-weekly threat information sharing calls for members and invited security/risk experts to discuss the latest threats, vulnerabilities and incidents affecting the sector;
- emergency threat or incident notifications to all members using the Critical Infrastructure Notification System (CINS);
- emergency conference calls to share information with the membership and solicit input and collaboration;
- engagement with private security companies to identify threat information of relevance to the membership and the sector;
- participation in various cyber exercises such as those conducted by DHS (Cyber Storm I, II, and III) and support for FSSCC exercises such as CyberFIRE
- development of risk mitigation best practices, threat viewpoints and toolkits, and preparation of cyber security briefings and white papers;
- administration of Subject Matter Expert (SME) committees including the Threat Intelligence Committee and Business Resilience Committee, which: provide in-depth analyses of risks to the sector, conduct technical, business and operational impact

assessments; determine the sector's cyber and physical threat level; and, recommend mitigation and remediation strategies and tactics;

- special projects to address specific risk issues such as the Account Takeover Task Force
- document repositories for members to share information and documentation with other members;
- development and testing of crisis management procedures for the sector in collaboration with the FSSCC and other industry bodies;
- semi-annual member meetings and conferences; and
- online webinar presentations and regional outreach programs to educate organizations, including small to medium sized regional financial services firms, on threats, risks and best practices.

FS-ISAC GOVERNMENT PARTNERSHIPS

The FS-ISAC works closely with various government agencies including the U.S. Department of Treasury, Department of Homeland Security (DHS), Federal Reserve, Federal Financial Institutions Examination Council (FFIEC) regulatory agencies, United States Secret Service, Federal Bureau of Investigation (FBI), National Security Agency (NSA), Central Intelligence Agency (CIA), and state and local governments.

For example, in partnership with DHS, FS-ISAC two years ago became the third ISAC to participate in the National Cybersecurity and Communications Integration Center (NCCIC) watch floor. FS-ISAC representatives, cleared at the Top Secret / Sensitive Compartmented Information (TS/SCI) level, attend the daily briefs and other NCCIC meetings to share information on threats, vulnerabilities, incidents, and potential or known impacts to the financial services sector. Our presence on the NCCIC floor has enhanced situational awareness and information sharing between the financial services sector and the government, and there are numerous examples of success to illustrate this.

As part of this partnership, the FS-ISAC set up an email listserv with U.S. CERT where actionable incident, threat and vulnerability information is shared in near real-time. This listserv allow FS-ISAC members to share directly with U.S. CERT and further facilitates the information sharing that is already occurring between FS-ISAC members and with the NCCIC watch floor or with other government organizations.

In addition, FS-ISAC representatives sit on the Cyber Unified Coordination Group (Cyber UCG). This group was set up under authority of the National Cyber Incident Response Plan (NCIRP) and has been actively engaged in incident response. Cyber UCG's handling and communications with various sectors following the distributed denial of service (DDOS) attacks on the financial sector in late 2012 and early 2013 is one example of how this group is effective in facilitating relevant and actionable information sharing.

Finally, it should be noted that the FS-ISAC and FSSCC have worked closely with its government partners to obtain over 250 Secret level clearances and a number of TS/SCI clearances for key financial services sector personnel. These clearances have been used to brief the sector on new information security threats and have provided useful information for the sector to implement effective risk controls to combat these threats.

FS-ISAC INDUSTRY PARTNERSHIPS

With respect to cooperation within the financial services sector, the FS-ISAC is a member of, and partner to the Financial Services Sector Coordinating Council (FSSCC) for Homeland Security and Critical Infrastructure Protection established under HSPD 7 and its successor PPD-21. We also work closely with other industry groups and trade associations that are members of the FS-ISAC including the American Bankers Association (ABA), Securities Industry and Financial Markets Association (SIFMA), Independent Community Bankers Association (ICBA), and the BITS division of the Financial Services Roundtable. In addition, our membership includes various payments, clearing houses and exchanges such as the National Automated Clearing House Association (NACHA), Depository Trust and Clearing Corporation (DTCC), New York Stock Exchange, NASDAQ, The Clearing House (TCH), the various payment card brands and most of the card payment processors in the U.S.

FS-ISAC has worked closely with the Regional Payments Associations to offer regional account takeover workshops for their members. These day-long events consist of presentations from defense in-depth solution providers and include an interactive tabletop exercise that engages the participants in a simulated series of cyber attacks against their financial institutions' customers.

In addition, several membership subgroups meet regularly with their own circles of trust to share information, including: the Insurance Risk Council (IRC); the Community Institution Council (CIC) with hundreds of members from community banks and credit unions; and the Community Institution Toolkit Working Group with a mission to develop a framework and series of best practices to protect community institutions. This includes a mentoring program to assist community institutions just getting started with an IT security staff.

One operation that has achieved measurable results is our partnership with Microsoft, with whom we twice collaborated over the last 3 years to identify and take down sophisticated "botnet" operations stealing from financial services companies and their customers. A botnet is in effect a network of computers ("bots") that have been hijacked by cyber criminals who are able to steal financial credentials such as account numbers, passwords and user ID's. Because the cyber criminals were using Microsoft's infrastructure, such as their email and web servers, to deliver malware to financial customers' computers, several financial sector organizations including FS-ISAC and Microsoft were together able to share information about the source and techniques of the attacks, and work under a court order with law enforcement to cut off the "command and control" of the so-called "bot herders". This succeeded in ending this particular criminal ring's operations and disinfecting millions of computers in collaboration with internet service providers.

The FS-ISAC also works very closely with the other critical infrastructure sectors on an ISAC to ISAC basis as well as through the National Council of ISACs. Information about threats, incidents and best practices is shared daily among the ISACs via ISAC analyst calls, and a cross-sector information sharing platform. The ISACs also come together during a crisis to coordinate information and mitigations as applicable.

A key factor in all of these activities is trust. The FS-ISAC works to facilitate development of trust between its members, with other organizations in the financial services sector, with other sectors, and with government organizations such as law enforcement, regulators, and intelligence agencies.

FS-ISAC AUTOMATED THREAT INTELLIGENCE STRATEGY

While trust relationships in any sensitive activity such as cyber information sharing are essential to a successful risk management strategy, we also recognize that "human-to-human" effort can be too slow when threats and attacks are happening at internet speed. For this reason, FS-ISAC has embarked on a substantial initiative to engage more "machine-to-machine" threat intelligence exchange in a way that will more quickly inform our financial infrastructure front line operators, and aid their preventive and incident response decision making.

Over the last 18 months, we've worked with members and other industry organizations to design the industry's first Cyber Threat Intelligence Repository to automate threat intelligence sharing for our members. A first of its kind, this solution collects, analyzes, prioritizes and shares threat information in near real-time within our sector. We are well on our way to delivering the first phases of this project, are investing heavily in development resources and have a compelling multi-year roadmap that will transform how threat information is shared.

Already, initial testing with open intelligence sources has collected a total of 6 million indicators. Version 1.0 was released to pilot users last year and Version 2.0 is expected to be released later in 2014 and will include capabilities like a federated sharing model with many local repositories as well as actionable intelligence down to a security controls level. We are working with vendors and other ISACs to extend the capability into other sectors.

Typically the time associated with chasing down any specific threat indicator is substantial. Our goal with this automation solution is to help our industry increase the speed, scale and accuracy of information sharing and accelerate time to resolution. This solution removes a huge burden of work for both large and small financial organizations, including those that rely on third parties for monitoring and incident response. With dozens of members participating in our first phase, we expect this automated solution to be a 'go to' resource to speed incident response across thousands of organizations in many countries within the next few years.

This concludes our written statement for the record. Thank you again for this opportunity to present this testimony and I look forward to your questions.

Payment Card Industry
Security Standards Council, LLC

401 Edgewater Place, Suite 600
Wakefield, MA 01880
Phone: 781 876 8855

Statement for the Record

Troy Leach
Chief Technology Officer
Payment Card Industry Security Standards Council

Before the Committee on Financial Services,
Subcommittee on Financial Institutions and Consumer Credit
United States House of Representatives

Data Security: Examining Efforts to Protect Americans' Financial Information

March 5, 2014
2128 Rayburn House Office Building

Introduction
Chairwoman Capito, Ranking Member Meeks, members of the subcommittee, on behalf of the PCI Security Standards Council, thank you for inviting us to testify today before the subcommittee.

My name is Troy Leach and I am the Chief Technology Officer of the Payment Card Industry (PCI) Security Standards Council (SSC), a global industry initiative and membership organization, focused on securing payment card data. Working with a global community of industry players, our organization has created data security standards—notably the PCI Data Security Standard (PCI DSS)—certification programs, training courses, and best practice guidelines to help improve payment card security.

Together with our community of over one thousand of the world's leading businesses, we're tackling data security challenges from password complexity to proper protection of PIN entry devices on terminals. Our work is broad for a simple reason: there is no single answer to securing payment card data. No one technology is a panacea; security requires a multi-layered approach across the payment chain.

The PCI Security Standards Council is an excellent example of effective industry collaboration to develop private sector standards. Simply put, the PCI Standards are the best line of defense against the criminals seeking to steal payment card data. And while several recent high profile breaches have captured the nation's attention, great progress has been made over the past seven years in securing payment card data through a collaborative cross-industry approach, and we continue to build upon the way we protect this data.

Consumers are understandably upset when their payment card data is put at risk of misuse and—while the PCI Security Standards Council is not a name most consumers know—we are sensitive to the impact that breaches cause for consumers. Consumers should take comfort from the fact that a great number of the organizations they do business with have joined the PCI SSC to collaborate in efforts to better protect their payment card data.

Payment card security: a dynamic environment

Since the threat landscape is constantly evolving, the PCI SSC expects its standards to do the same. Confidence that businesses are protecting payment card data is paramount to a healthy economy and payment process—both in person and online. That's why to date, more than one thousand of the world's leading retailers, airlines, banks, hotels, payment processors, government agencies, universities, and technology companies have joined the PCI Council as members and as part of our assessor community to develop security standards that apply across the spectrum of today's global multi-channel and online businesses.

Our community members are living on the front lines of this challenge and are therefore well placed, through the unique forum of the PCI Security Standards Council, to provide input on threats they are seeing and ideas for how to tackle these threats through the PCI Standards.

The Council develops standards through a defined, published three year lifecycle. Our Participating Organization members told us that three years was the appropriate timeframe to update and deploy security approaches in their organizations. In addition to the formal lifecycle, the Council and the PCI community have the resources to continually monitor and provide updates through standards, published FAQs, Special Interest Group work, and guidance papers on emerging threats and new ways to improve payment security. Examples include updated wireless guidance and security guidelines for merchants wishing to accept mobile payments.

This year, on January 1, 2014, our latest version of the PCI Data Security Standard (PCI DSS) became effective. This is our overarching data security standard, built on 12 principles that cover everything from implementing strong access control, monitoring and testing networks, to having an information security policy. During updates to this standard, we received hundreds of pieces of feedback from our community. This was almost evenly split between feedback from domestic and international organizations, highlighting the global nature of participation in the PCI SSC and the need to provide standards and resources that can be adopted globally to support the international nature of the payment system.

This feedback has enabled us to be directly responsive to challenges that organizations are facing every day in securing cardholder data. For example, in this latest round of PCI DSS revisions, community feedback indicated that changes were needed to secure password recommendations. Password strength remains a challenge—as "password" is still among the most common password used by global businesses—and is highlighted in industry reports as a common failure leading to data compromise. Small merchants in particular often do not change passwords on point of sale (POS) applications and devices. With the help of the PCI community, the Council has updated requirements to make clear that default passwords should never be used, all passwords must be regularly changed and not continually repeated, should never be shared, and must always be of appropriate strength. Beyond promulgating appropriate standards, we have taken steps through training and public outreach to educate the merchant community on the importance of following proper password protocols.

Recognizing the need for a multi-layer approach, in addition to the PCI DSS, the Council and community have developed standards that cover payment applications and point of sale devices. In other areas, based on community feedback, we are working on standards and guidance on other technologies such as tokenization and point-to-point encryption. These technologies can dramatically increase data security at vulnerable points along the transactional chain. Tokenization and point-to-point encryption remove or render payment card information useless to cyber criminals, and work in concert with other PCI Standards to offer additional protection to payment card data.

In addition to developing and updating standards, the PCI community votes annually on which topics they would like to explore with the Council and provide guidance on. Over the last few years the working groups formed by the Council to address these concerns have collaborated with hundreds of organizations to produce resources on third party security assurance, cloud computing, best practices for maintaining compliance, e-commerce guidelines, virtualization, and wireless security. Other recent Council initiatives have addressed ATM security, PIN security, and mobile payment acceptance security for developers and merchants.

EMV Chip & PCI Standards—a strong combination

One technology that has garnered a great deal of attention in recent weeks is EMV chip—a technology that has widespread use in Europe and other markets. EMV chip is an extremely effective method of reducing counterfeit and lost/stolen card fraud in a face-to-face payments environment. That is why the PCI Security Standards Council supports the deployment of EMV chip technology.

Global adoption of EMV chip, including broad deployment in the U.S. market, does not preclude the need for a strong data security posture to prevent the loss of cardholder data from intrusions and data breaches. We must continue to strengthen data security protections that are designed to prevent the unauthorized access and exfiltration of cardholder data.

Payment cards are used in variety of remote channels—such as electronic commerce—where today's EMV chip technology is not typically an option for securing payment transactions. Security innovation continues to occur for online payments beyond existing fraud detection and prevention systems. Technologies such authentication, tokenization, and other frameworks are being developed, including some solutions that may involve EMV chip—yet broad adoption of these solutions is not on the short-term horizon. Consequently, the industry needs to continue to protect cardholder data across all payment channels to minimize the ongoing risks of data loss and resulting cross-channel fraud that may be experienced in the online channel.

Nor does EMV chip negate the need for secure passwords, patching systems, monitoring for intrusions, using firewalls, managing access, developing secure software, educating employees, and having clear processes for the handling of sensitive payment card data. These processes are critical for all businesses—both large retailers and small businesses—who have become a target for cyber criminals. For smaller businesses, EMV chip technology will have a strong positive impact. But if small businesses are not aware of the need to secure other parts of their systems, or if they purchase services and products that are not capable of doing that for them, then they will still be subject to the ongoing exposure of the compromise of cardholder data and resulting financial or reputational risk.

Similarly, protection from malware-based attacks requires more than just EMV chip technology. Reports in the press regarding recent breaches point to the insertion of complex malware. EMV chip technology could not have prevented the unauthorized access, introduction of malware, and subsequent exfiltration of cardholder data. Failure of other security protocols required under Council standards is necessary for malware to be inserted.

Finally, EMV chip technology does not prevent memory scraping, a technique that has been highlighted in press reports of recent breaches. Other safeguards are needed in order to do so. In our latest versions of security standards for Point of Sale devices, (PCI PIN Transaction Security Requirements), the Council includes requirements to further counter this threat. These include improved tamper responsiveness so that devices will "self-destruct" if they are opened or tampered with, and the creation of electronic signatures that prevent applications that have not been "whitelisted" from being installed. Our recently released update to the standard, PTS 4.0, requires a default reset every 24 hours that would remove malware from memory and reduce the risk of data being obtained in this way. By responding to the Council's PTS requirements, POS manufacturers are bringing more secure products to market that reflect a standards development process that incorporates feedback from a broad base of diverse stakeholders.

Used together, EMV chip, PCI Standards, along with many other tools, can provide strong protections for payment card data. I want to take this opportunity to encourage all parties in the payment chain—whether they are EMV chip ready or not—to take a multi-layered approach to protect consumers' payment card data. There are no easy answers and no shortcuts to security.

Global adoption of EMV chip is necessary and important. Indeed, when EMV chip technology does become broadly deployed in the U.S. marketplace and fraud migrates to less secure transaction environments, PCI Standards will remain critical.

Beyond Standards – building a support infrastructure

An effective security program through PCI is not focused on technology alone; it includes people and process as key parts of payment card data protection. PCI Standards highlight the need for secure software development processes, regularly updated security policies, clear access controls, and security awareness education for employees. Employees have to know not to click on suspicious links, why it is important to have secure passwords, and to question suspicious activity at the point of sale.

Most standards organizations create standards, and no more. PCI Security Standards Council, however, recognizes that standards, without more, are only tools, and not solutions. And this does not address the critical challenges of training people and improving processes.

To help organizations improve payment data security, the Council takes a holistic approach to securing payment card data, and its work encompasses both PCI Standards development and maintenance of programs that support standards implementation across the payment chain. The Council believes that providing a full suite of tools to support implementation is the most effective way to ensure the protection of payment card data. To support successful implementation of PCI Standards, the Council maintains programs that certify and validate certain hardware and software products to support payment security. For example, the Council wants to make it easy for merchants and financial institutions to deploy the latest and most secure terminals and so maintains a public listing on its website for them to consult before purchasing products. We realize it takes time and money to upgrade POS terminals and we encourage businesses that are looking to upgrade for EMV chip to consider other necessary security measures by choosing a POS terminal from this list. Similarly, we are supporting the adoption of point-to-point encryption, and listing appropriate solutions on our website to take a solutions-oriented approach to helping retailers more readily implement security in line with the PCI standards.

Additionally, the Council runs a program that develops and maintains a pool of global assessment personnel to help work with organizations that deploy PCI Standards to assess their performance in using PCI Standards. The Council also focuses on creating education and training opportunities to build expertise in protecting payment card data in different environments and from the various viewpoints of stakeholders in the payment chain. Since our inception, we have trained tens of thousands of individuals, including staff from large merchants, leading technology companies and government agencies. Finally, we devote substantial resources to creating public campaigns to raise awareness of these resources and the issue of protecting payment card data.

The PCI community and large organizations that accept, store, or transmit payment card data worldwide have made important strides in adopting globally consistent security protocols. However, the Council recognizes that small organizations remain vulnerable. Smaller businesses lack IT staff and budgets to devote resources to following or participating in the development of industry standards. But they can take simple steps like updating passwords, firewalls, and ensuring they are configured to accept automatic security updates. Additionally, to help this population, the Council promotes its listings of validated products, and recently launched a program, the Qualified Integrator and Reseller program (QIR), to provide a pool of personnel able to help small businesses ensure high quality and secure installation of their payment systems.

The work of the Council covers the entire payment security environment with the goal of providing or facilitating access to all the tools necessary—standards, products, assessors, educational resources, and training—for stakeholders to successfully secure payment card data. We do this because we believe that no one technology is a panacea and that effective security requires a multi-layered approach.

Public – private collaboration

The Council welcomes this hearing and the government's attention on this critical issue. The recent compromises underscore the importance constant vigilance in the face of threats to payment card data. We are hopeful that this hearing will help raise awareness of the importance of a multi- layered approach to payment card security.

There are very clear ways in which the government can help improve the payment data security environment. For example, by championing stronger law enforcement efforts worldwide, particularly due to the global nature of these threats, and by encouraging stiff penalties for crimes of this kind to act as a deterrent. There is much public discussion about simplifying data breach notification laws and promoting information sharing between public and private sector. These are all opportunities for the government to help tackle this challenge.

The Council is an active participant in government research in this area: we have provided resources, expertise and ideas to NIST, DHS, and other government entities, and we remain ready and willing to do so.

Almost 20 years ago, through its passage of the Technology Transfer and Advancement Act of 1995, Congress recognized that government should rely on the private sector to develop standards rather than to develop them itself. The substantial benefits of the unique, U.S. "bottom up" standards development process have been well recognized. They include the more rapid development and adoption of standards that are more responsive to market needs, representing an enormous savings in time to government and in cost to taxpayers.

The Council believes that the development of standards to protect payment card data is something the private sector, and PCI specifically, is uniquely qualified to do. It is unlikely any government agency could duplicate the expansive reach, expertise, and decisiveness of PCI. High profile events such as the recent breaches are a legitimate area of inquiry for the Congress, but should not serve as a justification to impose new government regulations. Any government standard in this area would likely be significantly less effective in addressing current threats, and less nimble in protecting consumers from future threats, than the constantly evolving PCI Standards.

Conclusion

In 2011, the Ponemon Institute, a non-partisan research center dedicated to privacy, data protection, and information security policy wrote, "The Payment Card Industry Data Security Standard (PCI DSS) continues to be one of the most important regulations for all organizations that hold, process or exchange cardholder information."

While we are pleased to have earned accolades such as this, we cannot rest on our laurels.

The recent breaches at retailers underscore the complex nature of payment card security. A complex problem cannot be solved by any single technology, standard, mandate, or regulation. It cannot be solved by a single sector of society—business, standards-setting bodies, policymakers, and law enforcement—must work together to protect the financial and privacy interests of consumers. Today, as this committee focuses on recent damaging data breaches, we know that there are criminals focusing on committing or inventing the next threat.

There is no time to waste. The PCI Security Standards Council and business must commit to promoting stronger security protections while Congress leads efforts to combat global cyber-crimes that threaten us all.

We thank the Committee for taking an important leadership role in seeking solutions to one of the largest security concerns of our time.

###

Testimony of Edmund Mierzwinski

U.S. PIRG Consumer Program Director

at a hearing on

"Data Security: Examining Efforts To Protect Americans' Financial Information"

Before the House Financial Services Committee

Subcommittee on Financial Institutions and Consumer Credit

Honorable Shelley Moore Capito, Chair

5 March 2014

Testimony of Edmund Mierzwinski, U.S. PIRG Consumer Program Director at a hearing on "Data Security: Examining Efforts To Protect Americans' Financial Information," Before the House Financial Services Subcommittee on Financial Institutions and Consumer Credit, 5 March 2014

Chair Capito, Representative Meeks, members of the committee, I appreciate the opportunity to testify before you on the important matter of consumer data security. Since 1989, I have worked on data privacy issues, among other financial system issues, for the U.S. Public Interest Research Group. The state PIRGs are non-profit, non-partisan public interest advocacy organizations that take on powerful interests on behalf of their members.

Summary:

The authoritative Privacy Rights Clearinghouse has estimated that since 2005, fully 664,065,960 records have been breached in a total of 4,188 separate data breaches.[1] According to the Clearinghouse, the most recently reported breach is that Sears announced last Friday that the Secret Service is investigating Sears Holdings Corporation as a target of a similar security breach to the ones that hit Target and Neiman Marcus at the end of 2013. That recent exploit against Target Stores, depending on how it is measured, is among the largest ever.

Target, Neiman and other merchants should be held accountable for their failure to comply with applicable security standards but that does not mean they are 100% responsible for breaches. Merchants, and their customers, have been forced by the card monopolies to use an unsafe payment card system that relies on obsolete magnetic stripe technology, buttressed by a constantly changing set of so-called PCI standards to compensate for the inherent flaws of the underlying, ancient tech. When the mag stripe technology was used only for safer credit cards, this may have been acceptable, but since the banks and card networks have also aggressively promoted the use of debit cards on the unsafe signature (not safer PIN) based platform, consumer bank accounts have also been placed at risk.

Congress should carefully weigh its response to recent breaches. Increasing consumer protections under the Electronic Funds Transfer Act (EFTA), which applies to debit cards, to the gold standard levels of the Truth in Lending Act, which applies to credit cards, should be the first step. Facing higher liability may "focus the mind" of the banks on improving security. Second, Congress should not preempt the strongest state breach notification laws, especially with a federal breach law that may include a Trojan Horse preemption provision eliminating not only state breach laws, but all future state actions to protect privacy. That's the wrong response as we discuss below. Finally, Congress should also investigate the deceptive marketing of subscription-based credit monitoring and ID theft insurance products, which are over-priced and provide a false sense of security. In this case, although the highest risk to consumers is fraud on existing accounts, the modest credit monitoring product offered (for free) to Target customers will at best

[1] See "Chronology of Data Breaches," Privacy Rights Clearinghouse, last visited 4 March 2014 https://www.privacyrights.org/data-breach.

tell you that you have already become an identity theft victim. We make additional recommendations in the testimony below and are at all times available to brief committee staff or members.

The Target Breach (as an example):

The card information acquired in the first 40 million breached accounts that Target reported placed those debit/ATM or credit card customers at **risk of fraud on their existing accounts**. Because the scope of the records acquired in that RAM-scraping incident included not only the card number but also the expiration date, 3-digit security code (from the back of the card) and the (encrypted but probably hackable) PIN number or password, these numbers became very valuable on the underground market, as the Secret Service and Homeland Security have probably already explained. Subsequent reports on the Target breach indicate that the point of entry was a vendor's computer link for invoicing, and that that link allowed access to virtually all internal data systems, including those that contained the customer information.

In addition to RAM-scraping from the its store point-of-sale terminal systems, Target later admitted that additional information – including telephone numbers and email addresses – for up to a total of 70-110 million consumer records (some may have been the same consumers) held in a Customer Relations Management (CRM) database was also obtained, which places those customers **at the risk of new account identity theft.** Criminals will seek to obtain additional information, such as a consumer's Social Security Number, which would enable them to submit false applications for credit in your name.

When bad guys obtain emails and phone numbers, they make phishing attacks to obtain more information: While the email addresses and phone numbers are not enough information to commit identity theft, it is enough information to conduct such "phishing attacks" designed to collect additional information, including Social Security Numbers and encrypted passwords, from consumers.

They do this either through placing dangerous links in emails or using various "social engineering" techniques to trick you into providing more information. A phishing email will appear to be from your bank. But if you click on any links, either a virus explodes on your computer to collect any personal information stored on it, or you are redirected to a site that will allow them to obtain the information they need. Or, if they call you, they use the information that they have as a validation that they are from the bank, to trick you into providing the information that they need.

The additional information the bad guys seek, then, would either allow them direct access to your account (through the PIN) or to open new accounts in your name (with your Social Security Number) by committing identity theft. They use what they know to convince you to tell them what they don't know. They want your PIN, or your birthdate and Social Security Number. They hope to trick you into giving it up.

However, I believe the greater risk in this case is fraud on existing accounts, not identity theft. That is why so many banks re-issued debit and credit cards, or both, following the incident. But disappointingly, Target's main response to consumers – offering a free credit monitoring service – won't stop or warn of fraud on existing accounts. That provides consumers a false sense of security.[2]

It actually won't even stop identity theft, it will simply notify you after the fact of changes to your Experian credit report (but not to your Trans Union or Equifax reports, which may include different account information). Positively, the offered product terminates after one year, rather than auto-renewing for a monthly fee (when similar products were offered after some previous breaches, the over-priced, under-performing credit monitoring products were sometimes set to auto-renew for a fee).

Despite my reservations about Target's delayed and drawn out notifications to customers about the breach,[3] and its provision of the inadequate credit monitoring product, I don't believe that Target or other merchants deserve all of the blame for the data breaches that occur on their watch.

The card networks are largely at fault. They have continued to use an obsolete 1970s magnetic stripe technology well into the 21st century. When the technology was solely tied to credit cards, where consumers enjoy strong fraud rights and other consumer protections by law, this may have been barely tolerable.

But when the big banks and credit card networks asked consumers to expose their bank accounts to the unsafe signature-based payment system, by piggybacking once safer PIN-only debit cards onto the signature-based system, the omission became unacceptable. The vaunted "zero-liability" promises of the card networks and issuing banks are by contract, not law. Of course, the additional problem any debit card fraud victim faces is that she is missing money from her own account while the bank conducts an allowable reinvestigation for ten days or more, even if the bank eventually lives up to its promise.[4] Further, the contractual promises I have seen contain asterisks and exceptions, such as for a consumer who files more than one dispute in a year.

Further, the card networks' failure to upgrade, let alone enforce, their PCI or security standards, despite the massive revenue stream provided by consumers and merchants through swipe, or interchange, fees, is yet another outrage by the banks and card networks.

---

[2] Even worse, consumers who accept the monitoring product, protectmyid from the credit bureau Experian, must accept a boilerplate forced arbitration clause that restricts their ability to sue Experian. See http://www.protectmyid.com/terms/ And under current U.S. Supreme Court jurisprudence, that clause's outrageous ban on joining a class action is also permissible.

[3] I understand that some state Attorneys General are investigating whether adequate notification was made under their breach laws.

[4] Compare some of the Truth In Lending Act's robust credit card protections by law to the Electronic Funds Transfer Act's weak debit card consumer rights at this FDIC website: http://www.fdic.gov/consumers/consumer/news/cnfall09/debit_vs_credit.html

Incredibly, the Federal Reserve Board's rule interpreting the Durbin amendment limiting swipe fees on the debit cards of the biggest banks also provides for additional fraud revenue to the banks in several ways. Even though banks and card networks routinely pass along virtually all costs of fraud to merchants in the form of chargebacks, the Fed rule interpreting the Durbin amendment allows for much more revenue. So, not only are banks and card networks compensated with general revenue from the ever-increasing swipe fees, but the Fed allows them numerous additional specific bites of the apple for fraud-related fees.

To be sure, Target should be held accountable if it turns out, as has been reported, that it was not in compliance with the latest and highest level of security standards throughout its system. But understand that that system was inadequate at best because, like acting as any monopolists would, the card duopoly refused to make adequate technological improvements to its system, preferring to extract excess rents for as long as possible. For that reason, I cannot endorse any reform that makes Target, or other merchants, the only ones at blame. In many ways, the merchants are as much victims of the banks' unsecure systems as consumers are.

Recommendations:

1) Congress should improve debit/ATM card consumer rights and make all plastic equal:

Up until now, both banks and merchants have looked at fraud and identity theft as a modest cost of doing business and have not protected the payment system well enough. They have failed to look seriously at harms to their customers from fraud and identity theft – including not just monetary losses and the hassles of restoring their good names, but also the emotional harm that they must face as they wonder whether future credit applications will be rejected due to the fraudulent accounts.

Currently, debit card fraud victims are reimbursed at "zero liability" only by promise. The EFTA's fraud standard actually provides for 3-tiers of consumer fraud losses. Consumers lose up to $50 if they notify the bank within two days of learning of the fraud, up to $500 if they notify the bank within 60 days and up to their entire loss, including from any linked accounts, if they notify the bank after 60 days. However, if the physical debit card itself is not lost or stolen, consumers are not liable for any fraud charges if they report them within 60 days of their bank statement.

This shared risk fraud standard under the EFTA, which governs debit cards, appears to be vestigial, or left over from the days when debit cards could only be used with a PIN. Since banks encourage consumers to use debit cards, placing their bank accounts at risk, on the unsafe signature debit platform, this fraud standard should be changed.

As a first step, Congress should institute the same fraud cap, $50, on debit/ATM cards as exists on credit cards. (Or, even eliminate the cap of $50 in all cases, since it is never imposed.) Congress should also provide debit and prepaid card customers with the stronger billing dispute rights and rights to dispute payment for products that do not arrive or do not work as promised that credit card users enjoy (through the Fair Credit Billing Act, a part of the Truth In Lending Act).[5]

Debit/ATM card customers already face the aforementioned cash flow and bounced check problems while banks investigate fraud under the Electronic Funds Transfer Act. Reducing their possible liability by law, not simply by promise, won't solve this particular problem, but it will force banks to work harder to avoid fraud. If they face greater liability to their customers and accountholders, they will be more likely to develop better security.

2) Congress should not endorse a specific technology, such as EMV (technology of Chip and PIN and Chip and Signature). If Congress takes steps to encourage use of higher standards, its actions should be technology-neutral and apply equally to all players.

"Chip and PIN" and "Chip and signature" are variants of the EMV technology standard commonly in use in Europe. The current pending U.S. rollout of chip cards will allow use of the less-secure Chip and Signature cards rather than the more-secure Chip and PIN cards. Why not go to the higher Chip and PIN authentication standard immediately and skip past Chip and Signature? As I understand the rollout schedule, there is still time to make this improvement. Ask the bank and card network witnesses today for an explanation.

This example demonstrates why Congress should not embrace a specific technology. Instead, it should take steps to encourage all users to use the highest possible existing standard. Congress should also take steps to ensure that additional technological improvements and security innovations are not blocked by actions or rules of the existing players.

If Congress does choose to impose higher standards, then it must impose them equally on all players. For example, current legislative proposals may unwisely impose softer regimes on financial institutions subject to the weaker Gramm-Leach-Bliley rules than to merchants and other non-financial institutions.

Further, as most observers are aware, chip technology will only prevent the use of cloned cards in card-present (Point-of-Sale) transactions. It is an improvement over obsolete magnetic stripe technology in that regard, yet it will have no impact on online transactions, where fraud volume is much greater already than in point-of-sale transactions. Experiments, such as with "virtual card numbers" for one-time use, are being carried out online. It would be worthwhile for the committee to inquire of the industry and the regulators how well those experiments are proceeding and whether requiring the use of virtual card numbers in all online debit and credit transactions should be considered a best practice.

---

[5] For a detailed discussion of these problems and recommended solutions, see Hillebrand, Gail (2008) "Before the Grand Rethinking: Five Things to Do Today with Payments Law and Ten Principles to Guide New Payments Products and New Payments Law," Chicago-Kent Law Review: Vol. 83, Iss. 2, Article 12, available at http://scholarship.kentlaw.iit.edu/cklawreview/vol83/iss2/12

Further, as I understand it, had Chip and PIN (or Chip and Signature) been in use, it would not have stopped the Target breach, since unencrypted information was collected from the Target system's internal RAM memory, after the cards had already been used.

3) Investigate Card Security Standards Bodies and Ask the Prudential Regulators for Their Views:

To ensure that improvements continue to be made in the system, the committee should also inquire into the governance and oversight of the development of card network security standards. Do regulators sit on the PCI board? As I understand it, merchants do not; they are only allowed to sit on what may be a meaningless "advisory" board. Further, do regulators have any mandatory oversight function over standards body rules?

Recently, the networks have been in to see the Federal Reserve Board ostensibly to talk about interchange (swipe) fees. Since the Fed is not a witness today, the committee should ask the Fed and other prudential regulators about these matters at in letters or at any future hearings about these matters. In particular, ask the Fed to testify as to the purposes and discussions at these meetings held with the banks and card networks. Its summary of one of these meetings indicates that the issue was EMV (CHIP card technology) rollout:

> Summary (Meeting Between Federal Reserve Board Staff and Representatives of Visa, January 8, 2014) : Representatives of Visa met with Federal Reserve Board staff to discuss their observations of market developments related to the deployment of EMV (i.e., chip-based) debit cards in the United States. Topics discussed included an overview of their current EMV roadmap and Visa's proposed common application for enabling multiple networks on an EMV card while preserving merchant routing and choice.[6]

4) Congress should <u>not</u> enact any new legislation sought by the banks to impose their costs of replacement cards on the merchants:

Target should pay its share but this breach was not entirely Target's fault. The merchants are forced to use an obsolete and unsafe system designed by the banks and card networks, which, to make matters worse, don't uniformly enforce their additional often-changing security standards intended to ameliorate the flaws in the underlying platform. Disputes over costs of replacement cards should be handled by contracts and agreements between the players. How could you possibly draft a bill to address all the possible shared liabilities?

Of course, the Federal Reserve has already allowed compensation to banks for card replacement in circumstances where the Fed's Durbin amendment rule applies. It states:

> "Costs associated with research and development of new fraud-prevention technologies, card reissuance due to fraudulent activity, data security, card activation, and merchant blocking are all examples of costs that are incurred to detect and prevent fraudulent electronic debit transactions. Therefore, the Board has included the costs of these activities in setting the fraud prevention

[6] Available at http://www.federalreserve.gov/newsevents/rr-commpublic/pin-debit-networks-20131107.pdf

> adjustment amount to the extent the issuers reported these costs in response to the survey on 2009 costs."[7]

Under the Fed's Durbin rules the amount of this compensation is as follows: banks can also get 5 basis points per transaction for fraud costs, 1.2 cents per transaction for transaction monitoring, and 1 cent per transaction for the fraud prevention adjustment. Again, this is in addition to merchants already paying chargebacks for fraud as well as PCI violation fines, plus litigation damages.

5) Congress should not enact any federal breach law that preempts state breach laws or, especially, preempts other state data security rights:

In 2003, when Congress, in the FACT Act, amended the Fair Credit Reporting Act, it specifically did not preempt the right of the states to enact stronger data security and identity theft protections.[8] We argued that since Congress hadn't solved all the problems, it shouldn't prevent the states from doing so.

From 2004-today, 46 states enacted security breach notification laws and 49 state enacted security freeze laws. Many of these laws were based on the CLEAN Credit and Identity Theft Protection Model State Law developed by Consumers Union and U.S. PIRG.[9]

A security freeze, not credit monitoring, is the best way to prevent identity theft. If a consumer places a security freeze on her credit reports, a criminal can apply for credit in her name, but the new potential creditor cannot access your "frozen" credit report and will reject the application. The freeze is not for everyone, since you must unfreeze your report on a specific or general basis whenever you re-enter the credit marketplace, but it is only way to protect your credit report from unauthorized access. See this footnoted Consumers Union page for a list of security freeze rights.[10]

The other problem with enacting a preemptive federal breach notification law is that industry lobbyists will seek language that not only preempts breach notification laws but also prevents states from enacting any future data security laws, despite the laudable 2003 FACT Act example above.

---

[7] See 77 Fed. Reg. page 46264 (August 3, 2012), available at http://www.gpo.gov/fdsys/pkg/FR-2012-08-03/pdf/2012-18726.pdf.

[8] See "conduct required" language in Section 711 of the Fair and Accurate Credit Transactions Act of 2003, Public Law 108-159. Also see Hillebrand, Gail, "After the FACT Act: What States Can Still Do to Prevent Identity Theft," Consumers Union, 13 January 2004, available at http://consumersunion.org/research/after-the-fact-act-what-states-can-still-do-to-prevent-identity-theft/

[9] See http://consumersunion.org/wp-content/uploads/2013/02/model.pdf

[10] http://defendyourdollars.org/document/guide-to-security-freeze-protection

Simply as an example, S. 1927 (Carper) includes sweeping preemption language that is unacceptable to consumer and privacy groups and likely also to most state attorneys general:

SEC. 7. RELATION TO STATE LAW.

No requirement or prohibition may be imposed under the laws of any State with respect to the responsibilities of any person to—
(1) protect the security of information relating to consumers that is maintained or communicated by, or on behalf of, the person;
(2) safeguard information relating to consumers from potential misuse;
(3) investigate or provide notice of the unauthorized access to information relating to consumers, or the potential misuse of the information, for fraudulent, illegal, or other purposes; or
(4) mitigate any loss or harm resulting from the unauthorized access or misuse of information relating to consumers.

Most other bills before the Congress include similar, if not even more sweeping, abuses of our federal system, although HR 3990, "The Personal Data Privacy and Security Act of 2014," appears to have a narrower preemption scheme that may be intended to apply only to data breach notification.

At least one merchant I have spoken with told me: "Actually, Ed, it is relatively easy to comply with the different state breach laws. We haven't had a problem."

Such broad preemption will prevent states from acting as first responders to emerging privacy threats. Congress should not preempt the states. In fact, Congress should think twice about whether a federal breach law that is weaker than the best state laws is needed at all.

6) Congress Should Allow For Private Enforcement and Broad State and Local Enforcement of Any Law It Passes:

The marketplace only works when we have strong federal laws and strong enforcement of those laws, buttressed by state and local and private enforcement.

Many of the data breach bills I have seen specifically state no private right of action is created. Such clauses should be eliminated and it should also be made clear that the bills have no effect on any state private rights of action. Further, no bill should include language reducing the scope of state Attorney General <u>or</u> other state-level public official enforcement. Further, any federal law should not restrict state enforcement only to state Attorneys General.

For example, in California not only the state Attorney General but also county District Attorneys and even city attorneys of large cities can bring unfair practices cases.

Although we currently have a diamond age of federal enforcement, with strong but fair enforcement agencies including the CFPB, OCC and FDIC, that may not always be the case. By preserving state remedies and the authority of state and local enforcers, you can better protect your constituents from the harms of fraud and identity theft.

7) Any federal breach law should not include any "harm trigger" before notice is required:

The better state breach laws, starting with California's, require breach notification if information is presumed to have been "acquired." The weaker laws allow the company that failed to protect the consumer's information in the first place to decide whether to tell them, based on its estimate of the likelihood of identity theft or other harm.

Only an acquisition standard will serve to force data collectors to protect the financial information of their trusted customers, accountholders or, as Target calls them, "guests," well enough to avoid the costs, including to reputation, of a breach.

8) Congress should further investigate marketing of overpriced credit monitoring and identity theft subscription products:

In 2005 and then again in 2007 the FTC imposed fines on the credit bureau Experian for deceptive marketing of its various credit monitoring products, which are often sold as add-ons to credit cards and bank accounts. Prices range up to $19.99/month. While it is likely that recent CFPB enforcement orders[11] against several large credit card companies for deceptive sale of the add-on products – resulting in recovery of approximately $800 million to aggrieved consumers -- may cause banks to think twice about continuing these relationships with third-party firms, the committee should also consider its own examination of the sale of these credit card add-on products.

In addition to profits from credit monitoring, banks and other firms reap massive revenues from ID Theft insurance, sometimes sold in the same package and sometimes sold separately. Companies that don't protect our information as the law requires add insult to injury by pitching us over-priced monitoring and insurance products. The committee should call in the companies that provide ID theft insurance and force the industry to open its books and show what percentage of premiums are paid out to beneficiaries. It is probable that the loss ratio on these products is so low as to be meaningless, meaning profits are sky-high.

Consumers who want credit monitoring can monitor their credit themselves. No one should pay for it. You have the right under federal law to look at each of your 3 credit reports (Equifax, Experian and TransUnion) once a year for free at the federally-mandated central site annualcreditreport.com. Don't like websites? You can also access your federal free report rights by phone or email. You can stagger these requests – 1 every 4 months -- for a type of do-it-yourself no-cost monitoring. And, if you suspect you are a victim of identity theft, you can call each bureau directly for an additional free credit report. If you live in Colorado, Georgia, Massachusetts, Maryland, Maine, New Jersey, Puerto Rico or Vermont, you are eligible for yet another free report annually under state law by calling each of the Big 3 credit bureaus.

[11] We discuss some of the CFPB cases here http://www.uspirg.org/news/usp/cfpb-gets-results-orders-chase-bank-repay-consumers-over-300-million-over-sale-junky-credit

Although federal authority against unfair monitoring marketing was improved in the 2009 Credit CARD Act,[12] the committee should also ask the regulators whether any additional changes are needed.

9) Review Title V of the Gramm-Leach-Bliley Act and its Data Security Requirements:

The 1999 Gramm-Leach-Bliley Act imposed data security responsibilities on regulated financial institutions, including banks. The requirements include breach notification in certain circumstances.[13] The committee should ask the regulators for information on their enforcement of its requirements and should determine whether additional legislation is needed. The committee should also recognize, as noted above, that compliance with GLBA should not constitute constructive compliance with any additional security duties imposed on other players in the card network system as that could lead to a system where those other non-financial-institution players are treated unfairly.

10) Congress should investigate the over-collection of consumer information for marketing purposes. More information means more information at risk of identity theft. It also means there is a greater potential for unfair secondary marketing uses of information:

In the Big Data world, companies are collecting vast troves of information about consumers. Every day, the collection and use of consumer information in a virtually unregulated marketplace is exploding. New technologies allow a web of interconnected businesses – many of which the consumer has never heard of – to assimilate and share consumer data in real-time for a variety of purposes that the consumer may be unaware of and may cause consumer harm. Increasingly, the information is being collected in the mobile marketplace and includes a new level of localized information.

Although the Fair Credit Reporting Act limits the use of financial information for marketing purposes and gives consumers the right to opt-out of the limited credit marketing uses allowed, these new Big Data uses of information may not be fully regulated by the FCRA. The development of the Internet marketing ecosystem, populated by a variety of data brokers and advertisers buying and selling consumer information without their knowledge and consent, is worthy of Congressional inquiry.[14] **Thank you for the opportunity to provide the Committee with our views. We are happy to provide additional information to Members or staff.**

---

[12] The Credit Card Accountability, Responsibility and Disclosure (CARD) Act of 2009, Public Law 111-24. See Section 205.

[13] See the Federal Financial Institutions Examination Council's "Final Guidance on Response Programs: Guidance on Response Programs for Unauthorized Access to Customer Information and Customer Notice,"2005, available at http://www.fdic.gov/news/news/financial/2005/fil2705.html

[14] See the FTC's March 2012 report, "Protecting Consumer Privacy in an Era of Rapid Change: Recommendations For Businesses and Policymakers," available at http://www.ftc.gov/news-events/press-releases/2012/03/ftc-issues-final-commission-report-protecting-consumer-privacy. Also see Edmund Mierzwinski and Jeff Chester, "Selling Consumers Not Lists: The New World of Digital Decision-Making and the Role of the Fair Credit Reporting Act," 46 Suffolk University Law Review Vol. 3, page 845 (2013), also available at http://suffolklawreview.org/selling-consumers-not-lists/

William Noonan

Deputy Special Agent in Charge
United States Secret Service
Criminal Investigative Division
Cyber Operations Branch

Prepared Testimony

Before the
United States House of Representatives
Committee on Financial Services
Subcommittee on Financial Institutions and Consumer Credit

March 5, 2014

Good morning Chairman Capito, Ranking Member Meeks, and distinguished Members of the Subcommittee. Thank you for the opportunity to testify on the risks and challenges the Nation faces from large-scale data breaches of financial information, like those that have been recently reported which are of great concern to our Nation. The U.S. Secret Service (Secret Service) has decades of experience investigating large-scale criminal cyber intrusions, in addition to other crimes that impact our Nation's financial payment systems. Based on investigative experience and the understanding we have developed regarding transnational organized cyber criminals that are engaged in these data breaches and associated frauds, I hope to provide this committee useful insight into this issue from a federal law enforcement perspective to help inform your deliberations.

The Role of the Secret Service

The Secret Service was founded in 1865 to protect the U.S. financial system from the counterfeiting of our national currency. As the Nation's financial system evolved from paper to plastic to electronic transactions, so too has the Secret Service's investigative mission. Today, our modern financial system depends heavily on information technology for convenience and efficiency. Accordingly, criminals have adapted their methods and are increasingly using cyberspace to exploit our Nation's financial payment system by engaging in fraud and other illicit activities. This is not a new trend; criminals have been committing cyber financial crimes since at least 1970.[1]

Congress established 18 USC § 1029-1030 as part of the Comprehensive Crime Control Act of 1984; these statutes criminalized unauthorized access to computers[2] and the fraudulent use or trafficking of access devices[3]—defined as any piece of information or tangible item that is a means of account access that can be used to obtain money, goods, services, or other thing of value.[4] Congress specifically gave the Secret Service authority to investigate violations of both statutes.[5]

Secret Service investigations have resulted in the arrest and successful prosecution of cyber criminals involved in the largest known data breaches, including those of TJ Maxx, Dave & Buster's, Heartland Payment Systems, and others. Over the past four years Secret Service cyber crime investigations have resulted in over 4,900 arrests, associated with approximately $1.37 billion in fraud losses and the prevention of over $11.24 billion in potential fraud losses. Through our work with our partners at the Department of Justice (DOJ), in particular the local U.S. Attorney Offices, the Computer Crimes and Intellectual Property section (CCIPS), the International Organized Crime Intelligence and Operations Center (IOC-2), and others, we are confident we will continue to bring the cyber criminals that perpetrate major data breaches to justice.

[1] Beginning in 1970, and over the course of three years, the chief teller at the Park Avenue branch of New York's Union Dime Savings Bank manipulated the account information on the bank's computer system to embezzle over $1.5 million from hundreds of customer accounts. This early example of cyber crime not only illustrates the long history of cyber crime, but the difficulty companies have in identifying and stopping cyber criminals in a timely manner—a trend that continues today.

[2] *See* 18 USC § 1030

[3] *See* 18 USC § 1029

[4] *See* 18 USC § 1029(e)(1)

[5] *See* 18 USC § 1029(d) & 1030(d)(1)

The Transnational Cyber Crime Threat

Advances in computer technology and greater access to personally identifiable information (PII) via the Internet have created a virtual marketplace for transnational cyber criminals to share stolen information and criminal methodologies. As a result, the Secret Service has observed a marked increase in the quality, quantity, and complexity of cyber crimes targeting private industry and critical infrastructure. These crimes include network intrusions, hacking attacks, malicious software, and account takeovers leading to significant data breaches affecting every sector of the world economy. The recently reported data breaches of Target and Neiman Marcus are just the most recent, well-publicized examples of this decade-long trend of major data breaches perpetrated by cyber criminals who are intent on targeting our Nation's retailers and financial payment systems.

The increasing level of collaboration among cyber-criminals allows them to compartmentalize their operations, greatly increasing the sophistication of their criminal endeavors and allowing for development of expert specialization. These specialties raise both the complexity of investigating these cases, as well as the level of potential harm to companies and individuals. For example, illicit underground cyber crime market places allow criminals to buy, sell and trade malicious software, access to sensitive networks, spamming services, credit, debit and ATM card data, PII, bank account information, brokerage account information, hacking services, and counterfeit identity documents. These illicit digital marketplaces vary in size, with some of the more popular sites boasting membership of approximately 80,000 users. These digital marketplaces often use various digital currencies, and cyber criminals have made extensive use of digital currencies to pay for criminal goods and services or launder illicit proceeds.

The Secret Service has successfully investigated many underground cyber criminal marketplaces. In one such infiltration, the Secret Service initiated and conducted a three-year investigation that led to the indictment of 11 perpetrators allegedly involved in hacking nine major U.S. retailers and the theft and sale of more than 40 million credit and debit card numbers. The investigation revealed that defendants from the United States, Estonia, China and Belarus successfully obtained credit and debit card numbers by hacking into the wireless computer networks of major retailers — including TJ Maxx, BJ's Wholesale Club, Office Max, Boston Market, Barnes & Noble, Sports Authority and Dave & Buster's. Once inside the networks, these cyber criminals installed "sniffer" programs[6] that would capture card numbers, as well as password and account information, as they moved through the retailers' credit and debit processing networks. After the data was collected, the conspirators concealed the information in encrypted computer servers that they controlled in the United States and Eastern Europe. The credit and debit card numbers were then sold through online transactions to other criminals in the United States and Eastern Europe. The stolen numbers were "cashed out" by encoding card numbers on the magnetic strips of blank cards. The defendants then used these fraudulent cards to withdraw tens of thousands of dollars at a time from ATMs. The defendants were able to conceal and launder their illegal proceeds by using anonymous Internet-based

[6] Sniffers are programs that detect particular information transiting computer networks, and can be used by criminals to acquire sensitive information from computer systems.

digital currencies within the United States and abroad, and by channeling funds through bank accounts in Eastern Europe.[7]

In data breaches like these the effects of the criminal acts extended well beyond the companies compromised, potentially affecting millions of individual card holders. Proactive and swift law enforcement action protects consumers by preventing and limiting the fraudulent use of payment card data, identity theft, or both. Cyber crime directly impacts the U.S. economy by requiring additional investment in implementing enhanced security measures, inflicting reputational damage on U.S. firms, and direct financial losses from fraud—all costs that are ultimately passed on to consumers.

Secret Service Strategy for Combating this Threat

The Secret Service proactively investigates cyber crime using a variety of investigative means to infiltrate these transnational cyber criminal groups. As a result of these proactive investigations, the Secret Service is often the first to learn of planned or ongoing data breaches and is quick to notify financial institutions and the victim companies with actionable information to mitigate the damage from the data breach and terminate the criminal's unauthorized access to their networks. One of the most poorly understood facts regarding data breaches is that it is rarely the victim company that first discovers the criminal's unauthorized access to their network; rather it is law enforcement, financial institutions, or other third parties that identify and notify the likely victim company of the data breach by identifying the common point of origin of the sensitive data being trafficked in cyber crime marketplaces.

A trusted relationship with the victim is essential for confirming the crime, remediating the situation, beginning a criminal investigation, and collecting evidence. The Secret Service's worldwide network of 33 Electronic Crimes Task Forces (ECTF), located within our field offices, are essential for building and maintaining these trusted relationships, along with the Secret Service's commitment to protecting victim privacy.

In order to confirm the source of data breaches and to stop the continued theft of sensitive information and the exploitation of a network, the Secret Service contacts the owner of the suspected compromised computer systems. Once the victim of a data breach confirms that unauthorized access to their networks has occurred, the Secret Service works with the local U.S. Attorney's office, or appropriate state and local officials, to begin a criminal investigation of the potential violation of 18 USC § 1030. During the course of this criminal investigation, the Secret Service identifies the malware and means of access used to acquire data from the victim's computer network. In order to enable other companies to mitigate their cyber risk based on current cyber crime methods, we quickly share information concerning the cybersecurity incident with the widest audience possible, while protecting grand jury information, the integrity of ongoing criminal investigations, and the victims' privacy. We share this cybersecurity information through:

---

[7] Additional information on the criminal use of digital currencies can be referenced in testimony provided by U.S. Secret Service Special Agent in Charge Edward Lowery before the Senate Homeland Security and Governmental Affairs Committee in a hearing titled, "Beyond Silk Road: Potential Risks, Threats, and Promises of Virtual Currencies" (November 18, 2013).

- Our Department's National Cybersecurity & Communications Integration Center (NCCIC);
- The Information Sharing and Analysis Centers (ISAC);
- Our ECTFs;
- The publication of joint industry notices;
- Our numerous partnerships developed over the past three decades in investigating cyber crimes; and,
- Contributions to leading industry and academic reports like the Verizon Data Breach Investigations Report, the Trustwave Global Security Report, and the Carnegie Mellon CERT Insider Threat Study.

As we share cybersecurity information discovered in the course of our criminal investigation, we also continue our investigation in order to apprehend and bring to justice those involved. Due to the inherent challenges in investigating transnational crime, particularly the lack of cooperation of some countries with law enforcement investigations, occasionally it takes years to finally apprehend the top tier criminals responsible. For example, Dmitriy Smilianets and Vladimir Drinkman were arrested in June 2012, as part of a multi-year investigation Secret Service investigation, while they were traveling in the Netherlands thanks to the assistance of Dutch law enforcement. The alleged total fraud loss from their cyber crimes exceeds $105 million.

As a part of our cyber crime investigations, the Secret Service also targets individuals who operate illicit infrastructure that supports the transnational organized cyber criminal. For example, in May 2013 the Secret Service, as part of a joint investigation through the Global Illicit Financial Team, shut down the digital currency provider Liberty Reserve. Liberty Reserve is alleged to have had more than one million users worldwide and to have laundered more than $6 billion in criminal proceeds. This case is believed to be the largest money laundering case ever prosecuted in the United States and is being jointly prosecuted by the U.S. Attorney's Office for the Southern District of New York and DOJ's Asset Forfeiture and Money Laundering Section. In a coordinated action with the Department of the Treasury, Liberty Reserve was identified as a financial institution of primary money laundering concern under Section 311 of the USA PATRIOT Act, effectively cutting it off from the U.S. financial system.

Collaboration with Other Federal Agencies and International Law Enforcement

While cyber-criminals operate in a world without borders, the law enforcement community does not. The increasingly multi-national, multi-jurisdictional nature of cyber crime cases has increased the time and resources needed for successful investigation and adjudication. The partnerships developed through our ECTFs, the support provided by our Criminal Investigative Division, the liaison established by our overseas offices, and the training provided to our special agents via Electronic Crimes Special Agent Program are all instrumental to the Secret Service's successful network intrusion investigations.

One example of the Secret Service's success in these investigations is the case involving Heartland Payment Systems. As described in the August 2009 indictment, a transnational organized criminal group allegedly used various network intrusion techniques to breach security and navigate the credit card processing environment. Once inside the networks, they installed "sniffer" programs to capture card numbers, as well as password and account information. The

Secret Service investigation, the largest and most complex data breach investigation ever prosecuted in the United States, revealed that data from more than 130 million credit card accounts were at risk of being compromised and exfiltrated to a command and control server operated by an international group directly related to other ongoing Secret Service investigations. During the course of the investigation, the Secret Service uncovered that this international group committed other intrusions into multiple corporate networks to steal credit and debit card data. The Secret Service relied on various investigative methods, including subpoenas, search warrants, and Mutual Legal Assistance Treaty (MLAT) requests through our foreign law enforcement partners to identify three main suspects. As a result of the investigation, these primary suspects were indicted for various computer-related crimes. The lead defendant in the indictment pled guilty and was sentenced to twenty years in federal prison. This investigation is ongoing with over 100 additional victim companies identified.

Recognizing these complexities, several federal agencies are collaborating to investigate cases and identify proactive strategies. Greater collaboration within the federal, state and local law enforcement community enhances information sharing, promotes efficiency in investigations, and facilitates efforts to de-conflict in cases of concurrent jurisdiction. For example, the Secret Service has collaborated extensively with DOJ's CCIPS, which "prevents, investigates, and prosecutes computer crimes by working with other government agencies, the private sector, academic institutions, and foreign counterparts."[8] The Secret Service's ECTFs are a natural complement to CCIPS, resulting in an excellent partnership over the years. In the last decade, nearly every major cyber investigation conducted by the Secret Service has benefited from CCIPS contributions.

The Secret Service also maintains a positive relationship with the DOJ's Federal Bureau of Investigation (FBI). The Secret Service has a permanent presence at the National Cyber Investigative Joint Task Force (NCIJTF), which coordinates, integrates, and shares information related to investigations of national security cyber threats. The Secret Service also often partners with the FBI on various criminal cyber investigations. For example, in August 2010, a joint operation involving the Secret Service, FBI, and the Security Service of Ukraine (SBU), yielded the seizure of 143 computer systems – one of the largest international seizures of digital media gathered by U.S. law enforcement – consisting of 85 terabytes of data, which was eventually transferred to law enforcement authorities in the United States. The data was seized from a criminal Internet service provider located in Odessa, Ukraine, also referred to as a "Bullet Proof Hoster." Thus far, the forensic analysis of these systems has already identified a significant amount of criminal information pertaining to numerous investigations currently underway by both agencies, including malware, criminal chat communications, and PII of U.S. citizens.

The case of Vladislav Horohorin is another example of successful cooperation between the Secret Service and its law enforcement partners around the world. Mr. Horohorin, one of the world's most notorious traffickers of stolen financial information, was arrested on August 25, 2010, pursuant to a U.S. arrest warrant issued by the Secret Service. Mr. Horohorin created the first fully-automated online store which was responsible for selling stolen credit card data. Both CCIPS and the Office of International Affairs at DOJ played critical roles in this apprehension.

---

[8] U.S. Department of Justice. (n.d.). *Computer Crime & Intellectual Property Section: About CCIPS.* Retrieved from http://www.justice.gov/criminal/cybercrime/ccips.html

Furthermore, as a result of information sharing, the FBI was able to bring additional charges against Mr. Horohorin for his involvement in a Royal Bank of Scotland network intrusion. This type of cooperation is crucial if law enforcement is to be successful in disrupting and dismantling criminal organizations involved in cyber crime.

This case demonstrates the importance of international law enforcement cooperation. Through the Secret Service's 24 international field offices the Service develops close partnerships with numerous foreign law enforcement agencies in order to combat transnational crime. Successfully investigating transnational crime depends not only on the efforts of the Department of State and the DOJ's Office of International Affairs to establish and execute MLATs, and other forms of international law enforcement cooperation, but also on the personal relationships that develop between U.S. law enforcement officers and their foreign counterparts. Both the CCIPS and the Office of International Affairs at DOJ played critical roles in this apprehension. Furthermore, as a result of information sharing, the FBI was able to bring additional charges against Mr. Horohorin for his involvement in a Royal Bank of Scotland network intrusion. This type of cooperation is crucial if law enforcement is to be successful in disrupting and dismantling criminal organizations involved in cyber crime.

Within DHS, the Secret Service benefits from a close relationship with Immigration and Customs Enforcement's Homeland Security Investigations (ICE-HSI). Since 1997, the Secret Service, ICE-HSI, and IRS-CI have jointly trained on computer investigations through the Electronic Crimes Special Agent Program (ECSAP). ICE-HSI is also a member of Secret Service ECTFs, and ICE-HSI and the Secret Service have partnered on numerous cyber crime investigations including the recent take down of the digital currency Liberty Reserve.

To further its cybersecurity information sharing efforts, the Secret Service has strengthened its relationship with the National Protection and Programs Directorate (NPPD), including the NCCIC. As the Secret Service identifies malware, suspicious IPs and other information through its criminal investigations, it shares information with our Department's NCCIC. The Secret Service continues to build upon its full-time presence at NCCIC to coordinate its cyber programs with other federal agencies.

As a part of these efforts, and to ensure that information is shared in a timely and effective manner, the Secret Service has personnel assigned to the following DHS and non-DHS entities:

- NPPD's National Cybersecurity & Communications Integration Center (NCCIC);
- NPPD's Office of Infrastructure Protection;
- DHS's Science and Technology Directorate (S&T);
- DOJ National Cyber Investigative Joint Task Force (NCIJTF);
- Each FBI Joint Terrorism Task Force (JTTF), including the National JTTF;
- Department of the Treasury - Office of Terrorist Financing and Financial Crimes (TFFC);
- Department of the Treasury - Financial Crimes Enforcement Network (FinCEN);
- Central Intelligence Agency;
- DOJ, International Organized Crime and Intelligence Operations Center (IOC-2);
- Drug Enforcement Administration's Special Operations Division;
- EUROPOL; and

- INTERPOL.

The Secret Service is committed to ensuring that all its information sharing activities comply with applicable laws, regulations, and policies, including those that pertain to privacy and civil liberties.

Secret Service Framework

To protect our financial infrastructure, industry, and the American public, the Secret Service has adopted a multi-faceted approach to aggressively combat cyber and computer-related crimes.

Electronic Crimes Task Forces

In 1995, the Secret Service New York Field Office established the New York Electronic Crimes Task Force (ECTF) to combine the resources of academia, the private sector, and local, state and federal law enforcement agencies to combat computer-based threats to our financial payment systems and critical infrastructures. In 2001, Congress directed the Secret Service to establish a nationwide network of ECTFs to "prevent, detect, and investigate various forms of electronic crimes, including potential terrorist attacks against critical infrastructure and financial payment systems."[9]

Secret Service field offices currently operate 33 ECTFs, including two based overseas in Rome, Italy, and London, England. Membership in our ECTFs includes: over 4,000 private sector partners; over 2,500 international, federal, state and local law enforcement partners; and over 350 academic partners. By joining our ECTFs, our partners benefit from the resources, information, expertise and advanced research provided by our international network of members while focusing on issues with significant regional impact.

Cyber Intelligence Section

Another example of our partnership approach with private industry is our Cyber Intelligence Section (CIS) which analyzes evidence collected as a part of Secret Service investigations and disseminates information in support of Secret Service investigations worldwide and generates new investigative leads based upon its findings. CIS leverages technology and information obtained through private sector partnerships to monitor developing technologies and trends in the financial payments industry for information that may be used to enhance the Secret Service's capabilities to prevent and mitigate attacks against the financial and critical infrastructures. CIS also has an operational unit that investigates international cyber-criminals involved in cyber-intrusions, identity theft, credit card fraud, bank fraud, and other computer-related crimes. The information and coordination provided by CIS is a crucial element to successfully investigating, prosecuting, and dismantling international criminal organizations.

---

[9] *See* Public Law 107-56 Section 105 (appears as note following 18 U.S.C. § 3056).

Electronic Crimes Special Agent Program

A central component of the Secret Service's cyber-crime investigations is its Electronic Crimes Special Agent Program (ECSAP), which is comprised of nearly 1,400 Secret Service special agents who have received at least one of three levels of computer crimes-related training.

Level I – Basic Investigation of Computers and Electronic Crimes (BICEP): The BICEP training program focuses on the investigation of electronic crimes and provides a brief overview of several aspects involved with electronic crimes investigations. This program provides Secret Service agents and our state and local law enforcement partners with a basic understanding of computers and electronic crime investigations and is now part of our core curriculum for newly hired special agents.

Level II – Network Intrusion Responder (ECSAP-NI): ECSAP-NI training provides special agents with specialized training and equipment that allows them to respond to and investigate network intrusions. These may include intrusions into financial sector computer systems, corporate storage servers, or various other targeted platforms. The Level II trained agent will be able to identify critical artifacts that will allow for effective investigation of identity theft, malicious hacking, unauthorized access, and various other related electronic crimes.

Level III – Computer Forensics (ECSAP-CF): ECSAP-CF training provides special agents with specialized training and equipment that allows them to investigate and forensically obtain digital evidence to be utilized in the prosecution of various electronic crimes cases, as well as criminally-focused protective intelligence cases.

These agents are deployed in Secret Service field offices throughout the world and have received extensive training in forensic identification, as well as the preservation and retrieval of electronically stored evidence. ECSAP-trained agents are computer investigative specialists, qualified to conduct examinations on all types of electronic evidence. These special agents are equipped to investigate the continually evolving arena of electronic crimes and have proven invaluable in the successful prosecution of criminal groups involved in computer fraud, bank fraud, identity theft, access device fraud and various other electronic crimes targeting our financial institutions and private sector.

National Computer Forensics Institute

The National Computer Forensics Institute (NCFI) initiative is the result of a partnership between the Secret Service, NPPD, the State of Alabama, and the Alabama District Attorney's Association. The goal of this facility is to provide a national standard of training for a variety of electronic crimes investigations. The program offers state and local law enforcement officers, prosecutors, and judges the training necessary to conduct computer forensics examinations. Investigators are trained to respond to network intrusion incidents and to conduct electronic crimes investigations. Since opening in 2008, the institute has held over 110 cyber and digital forensics courses in 13 separate subjects and trained and equipped more than 2,500 state and local officials, including more than 1,600 police investigators, 570 prosecutors and 180 judges from all 50 states and three U.S. territories. These NCFI graduates represent more than 1,000 agencies nationwide.

Partnerships with Academia

In August 2000, the Secret Service and Carnegie Mellon University Software Engineering Institute (SEI) established the Secret Service CERT[10] Liaison Program to provide technical support, opportunities for research and development, as well as public outreach and education to more than 150 scientists and researchers in the fields of computer and network security, malware analysis, forensic development, training and education. Supplementing this effort is research into emerging technologies being used by cyber-criminals and development of technologies and techniques to combat them.

The primary goals of the program are: to broaden the Secret Service's knowledge of software engineering and networked systems security; to expand and strengthen partnerships and relationships with the technical and academic communities; partner with CERT-SEI and Carnegie Mellon University to support research and development to improve the security of cyberspace and improve the ability of law enforcement to investigate crimes in a digital age; and to present the results of this partnership at the quarterly meetings of our ECTFs.

In August 2004, the Secret Service partnered with CERT-SEI to publish the first "Insider Threat Study" examining the illicit cyber activity and insider fraud in the banking and finance sector. Due to the overwhelming response to this initial study, the Secret Service and CERT-SEI, in partnership with DHS Science & Technology (S&T), updated the study and released the most recent version just last year, which is published at http://www.cert.org/insider_threat/.

To improve law enforcement's ability to investigate crimes involving mobile devices, the Secret Service opened the Cell Phone Forensic Facility at the University of Tulsa in 2008. This facility has a three-pronged mission: (1) training federal, state and local law enforcement agents in embedded device forensics; (2) developing novel hardware and software solutions for extracting and analyzing digital evidence from embedded devices; and (3) applying the hardware and software solutions to support criminal investigations conducted by the Secret Service and its partner agencies. To date, investigators trained at the Cell Phone Forensic Facility have completed more than 6,500 examinations on cell phone and embedded devices nationwide. Secret Service agents assigned to the Tulsa facility have contributed to over 300 complex cases that have required the development of sophisticated techniques and tools to extract critical evidence.

These collaborations with academia, among others, have produced valuable innovations that have helped strengthen the cyber ecosystem and improved law enforcement's ability to investigate cyber crime. The Secret Service will continue to partner closely with academia and DHS S&T, particularly the Cyber Forensics Working Group, to support research and development of innovate tools and methods to support criminal investigations.

Legislative Action to Combat Data Breaches

While there is no single solution to prevent data breaches of U.S. customer information, legislative action could help to improve the Nation's cybersecurity, reduce regulatory costs on

[10] CERT—not an acronym—conducts empirical research and analysis to develop and transition socio-technical solutions to combat insider cyber threats.

U.S. companies, and strengthen law enforcement's ability to conduct effective investigations. The Administration previously proposed law enforcement provisions related to computer security through a letter from OMB Director Lew to Congress on May 12, 2011, highlighting the importance of additional tools to combat emerging criminal practices. We continue to support changes like these that will keep up with rapidly-evolving technologies and uses.

Conclusion

The Secret Service is committed to safeguarding the Nation's financial payment systems by investigating and dismantling criminal organizations involved in cyber crime. Responding to the growth in these types of crimes and the level of sophistication these criminals employ requires significant resources and greater collaboration among law enforcement and its public and private sector partners. Accordingly, the Secret Service dedicates significant resources to improving investigative techniques, providing training for law enforcement partners, and raising public awareness. The Secret Service will continue to be innovative in its approach to cyber crime and cyber security and is pleased that the Committee recognizes the magnitude of these issues and the evolving nature of these crimes.

Testimony of

Larry Zelvin
National Cybersecurity and Communications Integration Center Director
National Protection and Programs Directorate
U.S. Department of Homeland Security

Before the
United States House of Representatives
Committee on Financial Services
Subcommittee on Financial Institutions and Consumer Credit
Washington, DC

"Data Security: Examining Efforts to Protect Americans"

March 5, 2014

Introduction

Chairman Capito, Ranking Member Meeks, and distinguished Members of the Committee, I am here today to discuss the Department of Homeland Security's (DHS) roles in responding to the recently reported breach of point of sale (POS) systems at two major retailers and the apparent compromise of sensitive personal and financial information that resulted from those breaches. I will also put these actions in the context of DHS's responsibilities to deal with cyber threats to our Nation's financial transaction systems as well as other important elements of critical infrastructure.

During the recent POS system compromises, DHS's National Protection and Program Directorate's (NPPD) strong operational and private sector outreach programs were leveraged to help other retailers secure their systems to prevent future attacks while simultaneously supporting the United States Secret Service's (Secret Service) criminal investigation. The National Cybersecurity and Communications Integration Center (NCCIC) used its unique cybersecurity analysis and mitigation capabilities to coordinate efforts to secure systems against future attacks and provided timely analysis for the Secret Service. Through close coordination among DHS components and other partners, we have not only preserved the integrity of the Secret Service law enforcement investigation, we have provided businesses and users the key information they need to protect themselves and reduce the likelihood of a similar incident occurring in the future.

Today I'd like to review in greater detail how NPPD works daily with our colleagues at the Secret Service and with interagency and cross sector partners to respond to and mitigate this and other cyber incidents. I hope this overview will demonstrate the increasing importance of building and maintaining close relationships between law enforcement officials and network defense experts in order to address both the criminal aspects of malicious cyber activity, as well as to reduce continuing vulnerabilities, protect against future attacks, and mitigate consequences of incidents. The importance of effectively leveraging these complementary missions has been consistently demonstrated over the last several years, and is an increasingly important part of the broader framework used by the government and the private sector to cooperate responding to malicious cyber activity.

A Whole of Nation Approach to Cybersecurity

As the Department has highlighted in previous testimony, cyberspace is woven into the fabric of our daily lives. According to recent estimates, the Internet encompasses more than two billion people with at least 12 billion computers and devices, including global positioning systems, mobile phones, satellites, data routers, ordinary desktop computers, and industrial control systems that run the power plants, water systems, and much more that make up our nation's critical infrastructure. While this increased connectivity has led to significant transformations and advances across our country – and around the world – it also has increased complexity and exposes us to new vulnerabilities that can only be addressed by timely action and shared responsibility. The Nation's economic vitality and national security depend on a safe cyberspace where reasonable risk decisions can be made and the flow of digital goods, transactions, and online interactions can occur safely and securely. No country, industry, community or individual is immune to the threat of a cyber-attack and timely action is required to share necessary information in order to discover, address, and mitigate the ever-growing threat of malicious cyber activity.

Furthermore, no single agency or organization by itself can effectively respond to the rising threat of malicious cyber activity. Now, more than ever, there is a need for a civilian-government capability to engage not only with affected entities but with other critical infrastructure sectors and companies that also are at risk. Successful responses to dynamic cyber intrusions require coordination among DHS, the Department of Justice—including the Federal Bureau of Investigation, Criminal Division, National Security Division, and U.S. Attorneys' Offices—the Intelligence Community, the Department of State, the specialized expertise of Sector Specific Agencies such as the Department of the Treasury, private sector partners – who are critical to these efforts – and state, local, tribal and territorial, as well as international partners, each of which have unique roles to play. In carrying out these activities, NPPD promotes and implements a unified approach to cybersecurity incident response, which enables the efforts of a diverse set of partners. Our incident response activities are synchronized with the comprehensive and timely sharing of cybersecurity information, and done in a manner which ensures the protection of individuals' privacy, civil rights and civil liberties.

The Central Role of the National Cybersecurity and Communications Integration Center

To better manage and facilitate cybersecurity information sharing efforts, analysis, and incident response activities, exemplified by the recent retailer breach, the Department operates the National Cybersecurity and Communications Integration Center (NCCIC), an around-the-clock center where key government, private sector, and international partners all work together. The NCCIC is comprised of four branches: the United States Computer Emergency Readiness Team (US-CERT), the Industrial Control Systems Cyber Emergency Response Team (ICS-CERT), the National Coordinating Center (NCC) for Communications, and Operations Integration (O&I). These branches provide the capabilities, skills, knowledge, and partnerships needed to serve as a focal point for coordinating cybersecurity information sharing with the private sector; provide technical assistance, onsite analysis, mitigation support, and assessment assistance to cyber-attack victims; and coordinate the National response to significant cyber incidents affecting critical infrastructure.

While responding to the recent retailer compromises, the NCCIC specifically leveraged the resources and capabilities of US-CERT. US-CERT's global partnerships allow it to work directly with analysts from across multiple sectors and international borders to develop a comprehensive picture of malicious cyber activity and mitigation options. US-CERT's mission focuses specifically on computer network defense, and it is able to apply its full resources to supporting prevention, protection, mitigation, response, and recovery efforts. US-CERT publishes technical and non-technical information products assessing the characteristics of malicious cyber activity and improving the ability of organizations and individuals to reduce their risk.

US-CERT's unique ability to aggregate, analyze, and share diverse sets of information from law enforcement, the intelligence community, the private sector – including information sharing and analysis centers – and international partners through more than 200 CERT partnerships worldwide is critical to NCCIC's information sharing mission. Increasingly, our information sharing activities are undertaken using Structured Threat Information Expression (STIX), which allows for data to be shared at machine speed in a standard, machine readable format.

Current Threat Landscape and Recent Retail Company Targeting

The NCCIC currently sees malicious cyber activity perpetrated by a variety of actors who employ diverse methods to achieve their objectives.

For some time, cyber criminals have been targeting consumer data entered into POS systems. When consumers purchase goods or services from a retailer, the transaction is processed through POS systems, which consist of the hardware (e.g. the equipment used to swipe a credit or debit card and the computer or mobile device attached to it) as well as the software that tells the hardware what to do with the information it captures. When consumers use a credit or debit card at a POS system, the information stored on the magnetic stripe of the card is collected and processed by the attached computer or device.

The data stored on the magnetic stripe is referred to as "Track One" and "Track Two" data. Track One data is personal information associated with the account. Track Two data contains information such as the credit card number and expiration date. In some circumstances, criminals attach a physical device to the POS system to collect card data, which is referred to as "skimming". In other cases, cyber criminals deliver malware which acquires card data as it passes through a POS system, eventually exfiltrating the desired data back to the criminal.

POS systems are connected to computers or devices, and are often enabled to access the Internet and email services. Malicious links or attachments in emails as well as malicious websites can be accessed and malware may subsequently be downloaded by an end user of a POS system.

On December 19, 2013, a major retailer publically announced it had experienced unauthorized access to payment card data from the retailer's U.S. stores. The information involved in this incident included customer names, credit and debit card numbers, and the cards' expiration dates and card verification value security codes. Another retailer also reported a malware incident involving its POS system on January 11, 2014, that resulted in the apparent compromise of credit card and payment information. A direct connection between these two incidents has not been established.

In response to this activity, NCCIC/US-CERT analyzed the malware identified by the Secret Service as well as other relevant technical data and used those findings, in part, to create two information sharing products. The first product, which is publically available and can be found on US-CERT's website, provides a non-technical overview of risks to POS systems, along with recommendations for how businesses and individuals can better protect themselves and mitigate their losses in the event an incident has already occurred. The second product provides more detailed technical analysis and mitigation recommendations, and has been securely shared with industry partners to enable their protection efforts. NCCIC's goal is always to share information as broadly as possible, including by producing products tailored to specific audiences.

These efforts ensured that actionable details associated with a major cyber incident were shared with the private sector partners who needed the information in order to protect themselves and their customers quickly and accurately, while also providing individuals with practical recommendations for mitigating the risk associated with the compromise of their personal information. NCCIC especially benefited from close coordination with the Financial Services Information Sharing and Analysis Center during this response.

Ensuring Robust Privacy and Civil Rights and Civil Liberties Safeguards

Throughout our response to the retailer breaches we followed pre-existing protocols and control measures to protect personally identifiable information (PII) and other sensitive information that could cause harm to individuals or the critical infrastructure entities we provide assistance to. Our top level approach is to minimize the collection, retention, dissemination or use of PII, and other sensitive information that is not relevant to the cyber threat. There are also more detailed standards for handling specific types of information within specific programs and activities, tailored to the specific programs, the types of information handled and the mission requirements.

DHS remains committed to ensuring cyberspace is supported by a secure and resilient infrastructure that enables open communication, innovation, and prosperity while protecting privacy, confidentiality, and civil rights and civil liberties by design.

Public Outreach

It is important to note that the NCCIC is only one part of NPPD's overall effort to create a more secure cyberspace through working with private and public sector partners. NPPD continues to build its capabilities and our relationships by reinforcing the Department's Stop.Think.Connect.™ public awareness campaign, which is a year-round national effort designed to engage and challenge Americans to join the effort to practice and promote safe online practices. The Stop.Think.Connect.™ Campaign, launched during National Cyber Security Awareness Month in October 2010, helps Americans understand and manage the risks that come with living in a connected world. NPPD also works closely with the Secret Service

Electronic Crimes Task Forces, leveraging their public/private partnerships, and works closely with other Federal agencies, including Sector Specific Agencies, to share cybersecurity information with critical infrastructure owners and operators. We are aggressively pursuing the objectives of the Executive Order 13636, Improving Critical Infrastructure Cybersecurity, and Presidential Policy Directive 21, Critical Infrastructure Security and Resilience, to increase the quality, quantity and breadth of public/private sector information sharing, while remaining vigilant on privacy and civil liberties protections. This includes development of the EO 13636-directed voluntary program to support adoption of the NIST Cybersecurity Framework, by owners and operators of critical infrastructure and any other interested entities.

Conclusion

While the Secret Service's criminal investigation into the these activities is on-going, NPPD through the NCCIC and other organizations continues to build shared situational awareness of similar threats among our private sector and government partners and the American public at large. At every opportunity, the NCCIC and our private sector outreach program publish technical and non-technical products on best practices for protecting businesses and customers against cyber threats and provide the information sharing and technical assistance necessary to address cyber threats as quickly as possible.

Increased connectivity has led to significant transformations and advances across our country – and around the world. Our daily lives, economic vitality, and national security depend on the cyberspace. DHS, through NPPD programs and partnerships, including the NCCIC and its central role, is working to outpace the cyber threat in order to maintain security and thereby foster innovation that has resulted from this interconnectedness. I appreciate the opportunity to speak with you today about the progress that the NCCIC has made in response to an ever evolving cyber threat and the road ahead for future improvements to our nation's cybersecurity.

March 5, 2014

Statement for the Record

On behalf of the

American Bankers Association

before the

Subcommittee on Financial Institutions and Consumer Credit

of the

Financial Services Committee
United States House of Representatives

Statement for the Record

On behalf of the

American Bankers Association

before the

Subcommittee on Financial Institutions and Consumer Credit

of the

Financial Services Committee
United States House of Representatives

March 5, 2014

Chairman Capito, Ranking Member Meeks, and members of the Committee, ABA appreciates the opportunity to submit for the record comments regarding the recent Target and other data security breaches. The ABA represents banks of all sizes and charters and is the voice for the nation's $14 trillion banking industry and its two million employees.

The subject of today's hearing, *Data Security: Efforts to Protect Americans' Financial Information,* is an important one. Notwithstanding these recent breaches, our payment system remains strong and functional. No security breach seems to stop the $3 trillion that Americans spend safely and securely each year with their credit and debit cards. And with good reason: Customers can use these cards confidently because their banks protect them from losses by investing in technology to detect and prevent fraud, reissuing cards and absorbing fraud costs.

At the same time, these breaches have reignited the long-running debate over consumer data security policy. ABA and the thousands of community, mid-size, regional, and large banks we represent recognize the paramount importance of a safe and secure payments system to our nation and its citizens. We thank the Committee for holding this hearing and welcome the ongoing discussion. From ABA's perspective, Congress should examine the specific circumstances of the Target breach and the broader data security issues involved, and we stand ready as a resource to assist in your efforts.

In our statement for the record we will focus on four main points:

- **Protecting consumers is the banking industry's first priority.** As the stewards of the direct customer relationship, the banking industry's overarching priority in breaches like that of Target's is to protect consumers and make them whole from any loss due to fraud.

- **A National data breach standard is essential.** Consumers' electronic payments are not confined by borders between states. As such, a national standard for data security and breach notification is of paramount importance.

- **All players in the payments systems, including retailers, must significantly improve their internal security systems as the criminal threat continues to evolve.**

- **Protecting the Payments System is a Shared Responsibility.** Banks, retailers, processors, and all of the participants in the payments system must share the responsibility of keeping the system secure, reliable, and functioning in order to preserve consumer trust. That responsibility should not fall predominantly on the financial services sector.

Before addressing each of these points in detail, it is important to understand the data security vulnerabilities in our system. The numbers are telling and point to the need for shared responsibility to fight off the continual attacks on data.

I. Data Security: Where are the Vulnerabilities?

It is a sobering fact that, since January 2005, a total of over 4,200 breaches exposing almost 600 million records have occurred nationwide. (Source: Identity Theft Resource Center) There were over 600 reported data breaches during 2013 alone, an increase of 30 percent over 2012 and the third highest number of breaches over the last nine years. The two sectors reporting the highest number of breaches were the healthcare sector at 43 percent of reported breaches and the business sector, including merchants, which accounted for nearly 34 percent of reported breaches.

Moreover, the business sector, because of the Target breach, accounted for almost 82 percent of 2013's breached records. The Banking, Credit and Financial sector accounted for only 4 percent of all breaches and less than 2 percent of all breached records.[1] However, in spite of the small percentage of actual data breaches, the Banking, Credit and Financial sector bears a disproportionate share of breach recovery and fraud expenses. This is a consistent trend since 2005, where over this nine year period our sector accounted for approximately 8 percent of all reported breaches. The business sector accounted for approximately 36 percent and health care sector approximately 23 percent of all breaches over the same time period.

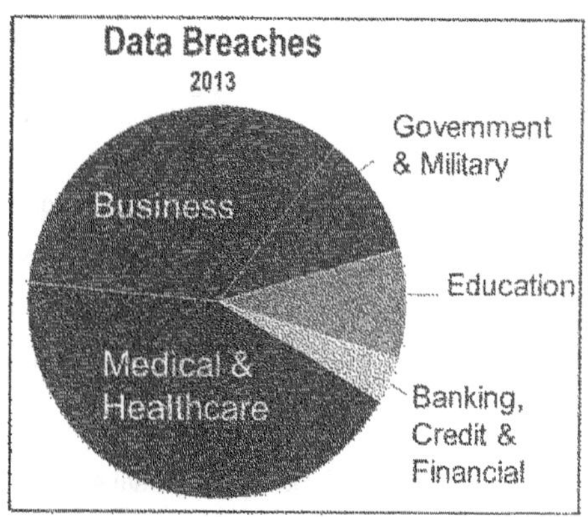

Source: Identity Theft Resource Center

These numbers point to the central challenge associated with breaches of financial account data or personally identifiable information: while the preponderance of data breaches occur at entities far removed from the banking sector, it is the bank's customer potentially at the end of the line who must be protected.

II. Protecting Consumers is Our First Priority

While the facts of the Target breach remain fluid, the company has acknowledged that the breach occurred within its internal systems, affecting nearly 40 million credit and debit card accounts while also revealing the personally identifiable information (e.g., name, address, email, telephone number) of potentially 70 million people. *On average, the Target breach has affected 10 percent of every bank's credit and debit card customer base.*

Paying for Fraud

When a retailer like Target speaks of its customers having "zero liability" from fraudulent transactions, it is because our nation's banks are making customers whole, not the retailer that suffered the breach. Banks are required to swiftly research and reimburse customers for

---

[1] *2013 Data Breach Category Summary*, Identity Theft Resource Center, January 1, 2014, Available at: http://www.idtheftcenter.org/images/breach/2013/BreachStatsReportSummary2013.pdf

unauthorized transactions, and normally exceed legal requirements by making customers whole within days of the customer alerting the bank of the fraud, if not immediately.[2]

After the bank has reimbursed a customer for the fraudulent transaction, it can then attempt to "charge-back" the retailer where the transaction occurred. Unfortunately, the majority of these attempts are unsuccessful, with the bank ultimately shouldering the vast majority of fraud loss and other costs associated with the breach. Overall, for 2009, 62 percent of reported debit card fraud losses were borne by banks, while 38 percent were borne by merchants.[3]

It is an unfortunate truth that, in the end (and often well after the breach has occurred and the banks have made customers whole) banks generally receive *pennies for each dollar* of fraud losses and other costs that were incurred by banks in protecting their customers. This minuscule level of reimbursement, when taken in concert with the fact that banks bear over 60 percent of reported fraud losses yet have accounted for less than 8 percent of reported breaches since 2005 is clearly inequitable. We believe banks should be fully reimbursed for the costs they bear for breaches that occur elsewhere.

Reissuing and Ongoing Monitoring

Each bank makes its own decision as to when and whether to reissue cards, which on average costs banks about $5 per card, but could be more. In the case of the Target breach, the decision of whether to reissue cards was made even more difficult considering the inconvenience this can cause during the holiday season: breach or no breach, many consumers would not have wanted their cards shut down leading up to Christmas. Those cards that have not been reissued are being closely monitored for fraudulent transactions. In some instances, banks gave customers an option of keeping their cards open through the holidays until they could reissue all cards in January or, if they were concerned, to shut their card down and be reissued a new card immediately.

---

[2] With traditional card payments, the rights and obligations of all parties are well-defined by federal statute when an unauthorized transaction occurs. For example, Regulation E describes consumers' rights and card issuers' obligations when a debit card is used, while Regulation Z does so for credit card transactions. The payment networks also have well-established rules for merchants and issuers. For instance, while Regulation Z limits a customer's liability for unauthorized transactions on a lost or stolen credit card to $50, the card networks require issuers to provide their cardholders with zero liability.

[3] *2009 Interchange Revenue, Covered Issuer Cost, and Covered Issuer and Merchant Fraud Loss Related to Debit Card Transactions*, June 2011, Board of the Governors of the Federal Reserve System, , available at: http://www.federalreserve.gov/paymentsystems/files/debitfees_costs.pdf

The Target compromise was also unique in terms of the high awareness of the "Target" name, the sheer number of people affected, and the media coverage of the event. In addition to proactively communicating with customers about the breach, bank call centers and branches have handled millions of calls and in-person inquiries regarding the card compromise. Many smaller and community banks have increased staffing to meet consumer demand. At the end of the day, consumers expect answers and to be protected by their bank, which is why they call us, not Target or whoever actually suffered the breach.

We also remain vigilant to the potential for fraud to occur in the future as a result of the Target breach. Standard fraud mitigation methods banks use on an ongoing basis include monitoring transactions, reissuing cards, and blocking certain merchant or types of transactions, for instance, based on the location of the merchant or a transaction unusual for the customer. Most of us are familiar with that call from a card issuer rightfully questioning a transaction and having a card cancelled as a result. In many cases, however, the lifespan of compromised consumer data extends well beyond the weeks immediately following the breach itself. Just because the headlines fade away does not mean that banks can afford to relax their ongoing fraud protection and screening efforts. In addition there are ongoing customer support issues as customer's setup new card numbers for recurring transactions related to health club memberships and online stores such as iTunes.

III. A National Data Breach Standard is Essential

In many instances, the identity of the entity that suffered the breach is either not known or, oftentimes, intentionally not revealed as there is no requirement to do so. Understandably, a retailer or other entity would rather pass the burden on to the affected consumers' banks rather than taking the reputational hit themselves. In such cases, the bank is put in the position of notifying their customers that their credit or debit card data is at risk without being able to divulge where the breach occurred. Many banks have expressed great frustration regarding this process, with their customers -- absent better information -- blaming the bank for the breach itself and inconvenience they are now suffering.

Like the well-defined federal regulations surrounding consumer protections for unauthorized credit or debit transactions, data breach notification for state and nationally-chartered banks is governed by guidance from the Federal Financial Institutions Examination Council (FFIEC), as enacted in the Gramm-Leach-Bliley Act, requiring every bank to have a customer response program. Retail establishments have no comparable federal requirements. In addition, not only are retailers, healthcare organizations, and others who suffer the majority of breaches not subject to federal regulatory requirements in this space, no entity oversees them in any substantive way. Instead they are held to a wide variety of state data breach laws that aren't always consistent. Banks too must also abide by many of these state laws, creating a patchwork of breach notification and customer response standards that are confusing to consumers as well as to companies.

Currently, 46 states, three U.S. territories, and the District of Columbia have enacted laws governing data security in some fashion, such as standards for data breach notification and for the safeguarding of consumer information. Although some of these laws are similar, many have inconsistent and conflicting standards, forcing businesses to comply with multiple regulations and leaving many consumers without proper recourse and protections.

Establishing a national data security and notification law, and requiring any business that maintains sensitive personal and financial information – including banks, verified-retailers, and data brokers – to implement, maintain, and enforce reasonable policies and procedures to protect the confidentiality and security of sensitive information from unauthorized use, would provide better protection for consumers nationwide.

Our existing national payments system serves hundreds of millions of consumers, retailers, banks, and the economy well. It only stands to reason that such a system functions most effectively when it is governed by a consistent national data breach policy.

IV. All Players in the Payments System Must Improve Their Internal Systems as the Criminal Threat Continues to Evolve

While many details of the Target breach are still largely unknown, it is clear that criminal elements responsible for such attacks are growing increasingly sophisticated in their efforts to breach the payments system. This disturbing evolution, as demonstrated by the Target breach, will require enhanced attention, resources, and diligence on the part of all payments system participants.

The increased sophistication and prevalence of breaches caused by criminal attacks – as opposed to negligence or unintentional system breaches is also borne out in a recent study by the Ponemon Institute. Evaluating annual breach trends, the Institute found that 2012 was the first year in which malicious or criminal attacks were the most frequently encountered root cause of data breaches by organizations in the study, at 41 percent.[4]

Emerging details of the Target breach are allowing us to see a troubling picture of the direction the criminal evolution is taking, and what it means for at-risk consumer data. For example:

- While Target's last public statement on the issue stated that the PINs that were compromised as part of the breach were encrypted, the company originally stated that PINs were not compromised at all. If the PINs were unencrypted, this would be particularly troubling, as that would make bank customer accounts vulnerable to ATM cash withdrawals as well as unauthorized purchases. We call on law enforcement and those in the forensics process to be as transparent as possible in outlining what are the precise threats to our customers.
- Even if the PINs that were breached were in fact encrypted, there is still the potential that they could be decrypted, placing our customers at just as much risk as if unencrypted PINs had been captured.
- Banks also do not know the extent to which their customers' bank account numbers, which are linked to Target's RedCard, were compromised as a result of the breach. If this information was compromised, customers could be vulnerable to unauthorized Automated Clearing House (ACH) transactions directly from their accounts.
- More generally, banks have also encountered significant customer confusion as to the nature of Target's RedCard and the bank's ability to help. Many believe the bank can cancel the card and reissue it even though the card was issued by Target. This confusion points to a broader problem with the emergence of many non-traditional payments providers: customers have a hard time understanding which payment entity is responsible for what, and often just assume the bank is the responsible party.

These threats to bank customer accounts point to the security vulnerabilities associated with non-traditional payments companies, such as Target, having direct linkages to the payments system without information security regulatory requirements comparable to that of financial institutions.

---

[4] *2013 Cost of Data Breach Study: United States*, May 2013, Ponemon Institute, available at: http://www.symantec.com/content/en/us/about/media/pdfs/b-cost-of-a-data-breach-us-report-2013.en-us.pdf?om_ext_cid=biz_socmed_twitter_facebook_marketwire_linkedin_2013Jun_worldwide_CostofaDataBreach

V. Protecting the Payments System is a Shared Responsibility

While much has recently been made about the on-going disagreements between the retail community and the banking industry over who is responsible for protecting the payments system, in reality our nation's payments system is made up of a wide variety of players: banks, card networks, retailers, processors, and even new entrants, such as Square, Google, and PayPal. Protecting this system is a shared responsibility of all parties involved and we need to work together and invest the necessary resources to combat increasingly sophisticated threats to breach the payments system.

We must work together to combat the ever-present threat of criminal activity at our collective doorstops. Inter-industry squabbles, like those over interchange, have had a substantial impact on bank resources available to combat fraud. Policymakers must examine that impact closely to ensure that the necessary resources are not diverted from addressing the real concern at hand – the security of our nation's payment system and the need to protect consumers. *All* participants must invest the necessary resources to combat this threat.

In the wake of this breach, there has been significant discussion over how to enhance payment card security, focusing on the implementation of chip-based security technology known as EMV.[5] This technology makes it much harder for criminals to create duplicate cards or make sense of encrypted data that they steal.

We encourage the implementation of chip technology, both on the card and at the point-of-sale. In fact, the rollout of this technology in the U.S. is well underway, with the next set of deadlines for banks and retailers coming in late 2015. It takes time for full implementation of chip technology in the U.S., as our country supports the largest economy in the world, with over 300 million customers, 8 million retailers, and 14,000 financial institutions.

Even though EMV is an important step in the right direction, there is no panacea for the ever-changing threats that exist today. For instance, EMV technology would not have prevented the potential harm of the Target breach to the 70 million customers that had their name, address, email, and/or telephone number compromised. Moreover, EMV technology will help to address potential fraud at the point-of-sale, but it does not address on-line security, nor is it a perfect solution even at the point-of-sale as criminal efforts evolve. Because it is impossible to anticipate what new

---

[5] EMV stands for Europay, Mastercard, and Visa, the developers of a global standard for inter-operation of integrated circuit, or "chip" cards and chip card compatible point-of-sale terminals and automated teller machines.

challenges will come years from now, we must therefore be cautious not to embrace any "one" solution as the answer to all concerns.

VI. The Path Forward

Any system is only as strong as its weakest link. The same certainly holds true in our rapidly-changing consumer payments marketplace. The innovations that are driving the industry forward and presenting consumers with exciting new methods of making purchases is also rapidly expanding beyond the bounds of our existing regulatory and consumer protection regimes. And, as has historically been the case, the criminals are often one step ahead as the marketplace searches for consensus. That said, there are several positive steps policymakers can take to facilitate a higher level of security for consumers going forward. For example:

Raise all participants in the payments system to comparable levels of security. Security within the payments system is currently uneven. In addition to adhering to the Payment Card Industry Data Security Standards, banks and other financial institutions are also subject to significantly higher information security requirements than others that facilitate electronic payments and house bank customer payment data.[6] More must be done to buttress and enforce the current regulatory requirements that merchants face.

Establish a national data security breach and notification standard. A national data breach standard, replacing the current patchwork of state laws and establishing one set of national requirements, would provide better and more consistent protection for consumers nationwide.

Make those responsible for data breaches responsible for their costs. Banks bear the majority of costs associated with the fraud caused by breaches even though our industry is responsible for only a small percentage of the breaches that have occurred since 2005. When any entity – be it a bank, merchant, college or hospital – is responsible for a breach that compromises customer payment data or personally identifiable information, that entity should be responsible for the range of costs associated with that breach to the extent it was not adhering to the necessary security requirements.

Increase the speed and transparency with which the results of forensic investigations are shared with the financial community. When a breach occurs, there is much banks and others do

---

[6] For instance, banks are subject to the information security requirements contained within the Gramm-Leach-Bliley Act, the FFIEC Red Flag Rules regarding identity theft, and are continually examined against these requirements.

not know and are not told for extended periods of time regarding the vulnerability of certain aspects of their customers' data. Similar to the robust manner in which banks and law enforcement currently share other cybersecurity threat data, we must examine ways to share the topline threat data from merchant and other breaches that does not impede the overall investigation. For example, banks and payment networks currently share an increasing amount of cybersecurity threat and fraud information through groups such as the Financial Services Information Sharing and Analysis Center and other groups within ABA. Our efforts would be greatly enhanced if that information sharing capacity expanded to include the merchant community. We would welcome such expansion and look forward to working collectively with merchants to combat our common adversaries.

Banks are committed to doing our share, but cannot be the sole bearer of that responsibility. Policymakers, card networks, and all industry participants have a vital role to play in addressing the regulatory gaps that exist in our payments system, and we stand ready to assist in that effort. Thank you for giving ABA the opportunity to provide this statement. We look forward to continuing to work with Congress to enhance the security of our nation's payment system, and maintain the trust and confidence hundreds of millions of Americans place in it every day.

Bill Cheney
President & CEO

March 5, 2014

The Honorable Shelley Moore Capito
Chairman
Subcommittee on Financial Institutions and Consumer Credit
United States House of Representatives
Washington, DC 20515

The Honorable Gregory Meeks
Ranking Member
Subcommittee on Financial Institutions and Consumer Credit
United States House of Representatives
Washington, DC 20515

Dear Chairman Capito and Ranking Member Meeks:

On behalf of the Credit Union National Association (CUNA) and America's credit unions, I am writing today to thank you for holding today's hearing entitled "Data Security: Examining Efforts to Protect Americans' Financial Information." CUNA is the largest credit union advocacy organization in the United States, representing America's 6,500 state and federally chartered credit unions and their 99 million members.

This hearing is an important and timely response to recent merchant data breaches affecting millions of Americans and their financial institutions. We appreciate the Subcommittee's focus on safeguarding consumer data, and we look forward to today's testimony and discussion of what should be done to ensure an appropriate response to not only the recent data breaches, but ones that may occur next week, next month, or next year. We encourage you to hold additional hearings on this matter to address the critical issues facing financial institutions that deal directly with consumers on these breaches.

As we noted in our February 19, 2014, letter to Chairman Hensarling and Ranking Member Waters, a prime reason that merchant data breaches are a chronic issue is because data security standards are inconsistent among the participants in the payments system. Simply put: credit unions and other financial institutions are subject to high data protection standards under the Gramm-Leach-Bliley Act; merchants are not. When merchant data breaches occur, financial institutions – not merchants – bear the costs of replacing credit and debit cards and fraud costs.

The witnesses at today's hearing will focus on how breaches like these happen, how future breaches might be prevented through the deployment of alternative technology and the impact that breaches have on consumers. While we welcome and appreciate this discussion, we are very skeptical that a solution to merchant data breaches can be achieved without addressing the inconsistency in data security standards. Further, until and unless merchants are held accountable for the damages that breaches to their systems cause financial institutions and consumers, we have little confidence that they will be incentivized to properly secure their systems. EMV, tokenization and other technologies are critical to the innovation of the payments system; however, the key role for Congress to play in addressing the issue of merchant data breaches is to make sure all of the participants are playing by the same set of rules, and that merchants that permit breaches to occur are responsible for the costs incurred by others.

Credit Unions and Other Card Issuers Are Paying the Price for Merchant Data Breaches

CUNA recently completed our annual Governmental Affairs Conference; merchant data breach was near the top of the list of concerns expressed by our more than 4,400 participants. It is an issue of such great concern because these breaches cost credit unions and their members significantly, and they divert resources from other credit union activity, including lending.

When a data breach occurs, credit unions immediately take steps to protect their members. They know what to do because they have had to do it all too often: they notify their members, make a determination of whether to reissue debit and credit cards, increase call center staff, set up account monitoring, and other activity. These steps are not without cost, however; and the impact of merchant data breach related costs is far reaching. For not-for-profit credit unions operating on already thin margins, these costs make a significant difference in their bottom line and therefore in their ability to offer services to their members.

CUNA recently conducted a survey of credit unions regarding the costs they are incurring to help their members respond and recover from the recent breach at Target. Based on 1,112 responses to CUNA's Target Breach Survey, representing between a third and 40% of credit union debit and credit cards, credit unions have thus far incurred estimated costs of $30.6 million. These costs have been predominately for card reissuance and other administrative expense resulting from the breach. Fraud losses, likely to be incurred in the future, will add to the total.

The survey shows that credit unions experienced increased call volumes and increased staffing as a result of the Target data breach. These added to the overall cost to credit unions. CUNA estimates that 4.6 million credit and debit cards were reissued. Credit unions reported two cost items related to the Target breach: card reissuance, and all other costs resulting from the breach (i.e. additional staffing, member notification, account monitoring, etc.). The averages of reported cards per affected card were:

- Card Reissuance: $3.23 per affected card
- All other costs: $2.46 per affected card
- Total costs: $5.68 per affected card

In summary, the data indicate that credit unions incur a cost of approximately $5.68 per affected card and that the credit union system has incurred a total estimated cost of at least

$30.6 million as a result of this breach. This figure will continue to increase because this data does not include fraud costs which may develop in the near future.

Looking to a historical example, in December, 2006, TJX Companies initiated an investigation after discovering suspicious software on its computer systems. The investigation found that for 18 months prior to the investigation, hackers had stolen information dating as far back as 2002 for more than 94 million credit and debit cards.[1] According to the Wall Street Journal, the breach happened as a result of poor wireless network security at the retailer.[2] According to court filings from October 23, 2007: "To date, Visa has calculated the fraud losses experienced by issuers as a result of the breach to be between $68 million and $83 million on Visa accounts alone." TJX entered into settlement agreements with Visa and MasterCard. Under the agreement, eligible card issuers received $40.9 million from Visa and $24 million from MasterCard. This equates to pennies on the dollar for credit unions who reissued debit and credit cards and did nothing wrong.

Congress Needs to Hold Merchants to the Same Standard as Financial Institutions

Data breaches occur, in part, because merchants are not required to adhere to the same Federal statutory data security standards that credit unions and other financial institutions must follow, and merchants are rarely held accountable for the costs others incur as a result of the breaches. All participants in the payment process have a shared responsibility to protect consumer data, but the law and the incentive structure today allows merchants to abdicate that responsibility, making consumers vulnerable.

In addition to the actual costs credit unions must bear as a result of the breach, credit unions also face reputational damage because they have an obligation to notify their members that their account has been compromised but are often limited in their ability to disclose the name of the merchant where the breach occurred. So, when members are notified that their account has been compromised, the credit union may not be able to tell them where the compromise occurred and some members may assume the problem occurred at the credit union.

As Congress considers legislative remedies, credit unions support three basic principles:

1. All participants in the payments system should be responsible and be held to comparable levels of Federal data security requirements.

---

[1]http://www.pillsburylaw.com/publications/tj-maxx-settlement-requires-creation-of-information-security-program-and-funding-of-state-data-protection-and-prosecution-efforts

[2] Wall Street Journal: "How Credit-Card Data Went Out Wireless Door." http://online.wsj.com/news/articles/SB117824446226991797. 4 May 2007.

Under current federal law, credit unions and other financial institutions are held to high standards of data security for consumer information under the *Gramm-Leach-Bliley Act*. There is no comparable federal data security responsibility for a national merchant holding consumer data. This represents a weak link in the chain and it needs to be addressed.

2. Those responsible for the data breach should be responsible for the costs of helping consumers.

It has been said by merchants that consumers will not be responsible for any financial loss in their accounts. That is true, but not because the merchant will reimburse affected consumers or assist them with their cards. It happens because the consumer's financial institution pays for the costs related to a merchant data breach involving accounts held at that institution. Under current law, the merchant is not obligated to reimburse financial institutions for any costs incurred as a result of the breach. In other words, even though the breach happened on the merchant's watch, retailers have no responsibility for the costs of the breach because financial institutions are the ones who take care of their members and customers.

When a merchant data breach occurs, credit unions are there to help their members. Whether it is increased staffing to handle additional member questions, notifying members, reissuing cards, tracking possible fraudulent activity, or reimbursing a member for fraudulent charges caused by a third party, credit unions bear the costs even though the merchant was responsible for the breach. We support legislation to address this problem and make it easier for credit unions to recoup the costs they incur. We believe that if Congress sets strong merchant data security standards and those standards are not met by a merchant whose data is breached, the merchant should be held responsible for the credit union's costs associated with that breach.

3. Consumers should know where their information was breached.

Credit unions also support legislation that requires merchants to provide notice to those consumers affected by a data breach, and permits credit unions to disclose where a breach occurs when notifying members that their account has been compromised.

When it comes to bad news like a data breach, it is easy to "blame the messenger." In today's world, the credit union is the messenger and, depending on state law and other agreements, may not be permitted to identify the breach source to the consumer member. Consumers need transparency and knowledge to understand where their data has been put at risk.

Conclusion

Target and Neiman Marcus will not be the last merchant data breaches to capture the headlines unless Congress takes strong steps to enhance data security standards for merchants that accept payment cards. We appreciate that the Subcommittee has an important responsibility to provide leadership in this area, and we will continue to highlight the impact that these breaches have on credit unions and their members as the Subcommittee pursues a remedy to this critical issue.

On behalf of America's credit unions and their 99 million members, thank you for your attention to this very critical matter and your consideration of our views.

Best regards,

Bill Cheney
President & CEO

March 5, 2014

Retailer Data Breach: The Community Bank Perspective

On behalf of the nearly 7,000 community banks represented by the Independent Community Bankers of America (ICBA), thank you for convening today's hearing titled: "Data Security: Examining Efforts to Protect Americans' Financial Information." Community bankers and their customers are deeply alarmed by recent, wide-scale data breaches at prominent, national retail chains. These breaches have the potential to jeopardize consumers' financial integrity and confidence in the payments system. This confidence is vital to sustaining consumer spending necessary for the economic recovery. It is critical we determine what happened, identify the weakest links in the payments processing chain, and implement targeted changes to enhance consumer financial data security. We appreciate the opportunity to offer the community bank perspective on this important issue.

Making Customers Whole

In the wake of the retailer breaches, community banks have reissued more than four million credit and debit cards to consumers at a total reissuance cost of more than $40 million.[1] Reissuance costs are higher for community banks than for larger institutions that are able to take advantage of economies of scale. Community banks absorb these costs upfront, even though the breaches occurred with retailers, because their primary concern is to protect their customers. Ultimately, these costs should be borne by the party that experiences the breach. This change would strengthen incentives for data protection. Because community banks acted quickly, initial fraud costs were relatively low. Less than one percent of community bank customers reported fraud on their accounts as a result of the recent breaches. These consumers are protected by a policy of zero-liability coverage. Financial institutions are required to provide this protection in order to issue Visa and MasterCard debit and credit cards.

While our current focus is on making customers whole, it is appropriate to begin to consider changes in policy, business practices, and technology that will strengthen payment system security and curb the risk of future breaches. The Joint Cybersecurity Partnership, linking ICBA and other financial services and retailer trade organizations, holds the promise of strengthening much needed cooperation across the payments chain.

More Comprehensive Data Security Standards Are Needed

Since 1999, financial institutions have been subject to rigorous data protection standards under the Gramm-Leach-Bliley Act (GLBA). These standards have been effective in securing consumer data at financial institutions. To adequately protect consumers and the payments system, **all** participants in the payments system should be subject to GLBA-like standards. Under current law, merchants and other parties that process or store consumer financial data are not

---

[1] Numbers are based on a survey of community banks.

subject to federal data security standards. Securing financial data at banks is of limited value if it remains exposed at point-of-sale and other points along the processing system.

Liability Should Be Used To Align Incentives

To maximize data security, the party that experiences a breach should bear responsibility for all costs associated with the breach. This change would better align incentives to keep consumer data safe and foster good business practices. As described above, when payment card information is compromised, mitigation costs are significant. If the party that experiences the breach does not bear these costs, they have little incentive to improve their data security.

National Data Security Breach and Notification Standard is Vital

Most states have enacted laws with differing requirements for protecting customer information and giving noticein the event of a data breach. This patchwork of state laws only increases burdens and costs, fosters confusion, and ultimately is detrimental to customers. Customer notification is important so that customers can take steps to protect themselves from identity theft or fraud. However, notification requirements should provide financial institutions and others with the flexibility to determine when notice is useful and appropriate. An overly broad notification standard that requires notice even when no threat exists will blunt the impact of notices that signal actual risk. Federal banking agencies should continue to set these standards for financial institutions.

Information Sharing Essential to Threat Reduction

Information sharing between law enforcement and the financial and retail sectors is an essential component of efforts to enhance customer data security. Unnecessary barriers to effective threat information sharing should be removed.

New Technologies Will Reduce Risk But There Is No Universal Remedy

Community banks are already investing in technologies that will better secure transaction processing and help thwart criminals. In particular, community banks are joining other financial institutions in the orderly migration to chip technology for debit and credit cards. Chip technology may not have prevented the recent retailer breaches but it would have reduced the market value of the card data as it would be far more difficult for criminals to make counterfeit cards. Chip technology will not protect against fraud in "card-not-present" transactions, such as online purchases. Criminals will continue to try to find weaknesses, regardless of the technology, so it is crucial that the marketplace continues to have the flexibility to innovate.

Thank you again for convening this hearing. ICBA looks forward to working with this Committee to craft targeted solutions to enhance the security of consumer financial data.

3138 10th Street North
Arlington, VA 22201-2149
703.522.4770 | 800.336.4644
F: 703.524.1082
nafcu@nafcu.org
National Association of Federal Credit Unions | www.nafcu.org

March 4, 2014

The Honorable Shelley Moore Capito
Chairman
Subcommittee on Financial Institutions
and Consumer Credit
House Financial Services Committee
United States House of Representatives
Washington, D.C. 20515

The Honorable Gregory Meeks
Ranking Member
Subcommittee on Financial Institutions
and Consumer Credit
House Financial Services Committee
United States House of Representatives
Washington, D.C. 20515

Re: Data Security: Examining Efforts to Protect Americans' Financial Information

Dear Chairman Capito and Ranking Member Meeks:

On behalf of the National Association of Federal Credit Unions, the only trade association exclusively representing the interests of our nation's federally chartered credit unions, I write today in advance of tomorrow's subcommittee hearing, "Data Security: Examining Efforts to Protect Americans' Financial Information." Data security is a chief priority of NAFCU member credit unions and the 97 million credit union members they serve. We appreciate the opportunity to share our concerns with you and look forward to the exploration of the impact of ongoing data breaches on consumers, as well as the community-based financial institutions that serve them.

Unfortunately, large national data breaches are becoming all too common. In just the last few months, consumers and credit unions have not only been affected by the recent Target Corporation breach, but also with additional national breaches at Neiman Marcus, Michaels and the White Lodging hotel management company. Tens of millions of Americans have been adversely impacted by these breaches. While these breaches draw national attention, many other "smaller" breaches are having just as much impact on the American consumer.

A January 2014, survey of NAFCU-member credit unions found that, on average, credit unions were notified over 100 times in 2013, of possible breaches of their members' financial information. That same survey found that nearly 80% of the time those notifications led to the credit union issuing a new plastic card to the member at their request because of the security breach, at an average cost of $5.00 to $15.00 per card.

The recent Target breach has been especially onerous on credit unions. Our member credit unions report that, on average, they have received hundreds of inquiries from their members seeking assistance due to the recent Target breach. NAFCU estimates that this particular breach could end up costing the credit union community nearly $30 million. This cost comes from fraud monitoring, reissuance of cards and actual losses from this breach. It does not even count the intangible cost of the staff time needed to handle all of the member service issues that stem from the breach. Unfortunately, credit unions will likely never recoup much of this cost, as there is no statutory requirement on merchants to be accountable for costs associated with breaches that result on their end.

These numbers echo what has historically happened to credit unions when a major retailer data breach occurs. A recent survey of NAFCU-member credit unions found that the 2006, data breach at TJ Maxx stores led to a median cost of $32,000 per institution from the breach, with only about 10% of those costs ever recovered on average.

As we first wrote to Congress in February 2013, as part of NAFCU's five-point plan on regulatory relief, these incidents must be addressed by lawmakers. Every time consumers choose to use plastic cards for payments at a register or make online payments from their accounts, they unwittingly put themselves at risk. Many are not aware that their financial and personal identities could be stolen or that fraudulent charges could appear on their accounts, in turn damaging their credit scores and reputations. Consumers trust that entities collecting this type of information will, at the very least, make a minimal effort to protect them from such risks. Unfortunately, this is not always true.

Financial institutions, including credit unions, have been subject to standards on data security since the passage of *Gramm-Leach-Bliley.* However, retailers and many other entities that handle sensitive personal financial data are not subject to these same standards, and they become victims of data breaches and data theft all too often. While these entities still get paid, financial institutions bear a significant burden as the issuers of payment cards used by millions of consumers. Credit unions suffer steep losses in re-establishing member safety after a data breach occurs. They are often forced to charge off fraud-related losses, many of which stem from a negligent entity's failure to protect sensitive financial and personal information or the illegal maintenance of such information in their systems. Moreover, as many cases of identity theft have been attributed to data breaches, and as identity theft continues to rise, any entity that stores financial or personally identifiable information should be held to minimum standards for protecting such data.

While some argue for financial institutions to expedite a switch to a "chip and pin" card, the reality is that chip and pin is no panacea for data security and preventing merchant data breaches. Many financial institutions that issue chip and pin cards had those cards stolen in the Target data breach, as the retailer only accepted magnetic stripe technology at the point of sale where the breach occurred. Furthermore, chip and pin cards can be compromised and used in online purchase fraud. This fact highlights the need for greater national data security standards as the way to truly help protect consumer financial information.

Again, recent breaches are just the latest in a string of large-scale data breaches impacting millions of American consumers. The aftermath of these and previous breaches demonstrate what we have been communicating to Congress all along: credit unions and other financial institutions – not retailers and other entities – are out in front protecting consumers, picking up the pieces after a data breach occurs. It is the credit union or other financial institution that must notify its account holders, issue new cards, replenish stolen funds, change account numbers and accommodate increased customer service demands that inevitably follow a major data breach. Unfortunately, too often the negligent entity that caused these expenses by failing to protect consumer data loses nothing and is often undisclosed to the consumer.

NAFCU specifically recommends that Congress make it a priority to craft legislation and act on the following issues related to data security:

- **Payment of Breach Costs by Breached Entities:** NAFCU asks that credit union expenditures for breaches resulting from card use be reduced. A reasonable and equitable way of addressing this concern would be to require entities to be accountable for costs of data breaches that result on their end, especially when their own negligence is to blame.

- **National Standards for Safekeeping Information:** It is critical that sensitive personal information be safeguarded at all stages of transmission. Under Gramm-Leach-Bliley, credit unions and other financial institutions are required to meet certain criteria for safekeeping consumers' personal information. Unfortunately, there is no comprehensive regulatory structure akin to Gramm-Leach-Bliley that covers retailers, merchants and others who collect and hold sensitive information. NAFCU strongly supports the passage of legislation requiring any entity responsible for the storage of consumer data to meet standards similar to those imposed on financial institutions under the Gramm-Leach-Bliley Act.

- **Data Security Policy Disclosure:** Many consumers are unaware of the risks they are exposed to when they provide their personal information. NAFCU believes this problem can be alleviated by simply requiring merchants to post their data security policies at the point of sale if they take sensitive financial data. Such a disclosure requirement would come at little or no cost to the merchant but would provide an important benefit to the public at large.

- **Notification of the Account Servicer:** The account servicer or owner is in the unique position of being able to monitor for suspicious activity and prevent fraudulent transactions before they occur. NAFCU believes that it would make sense to include entities such as financial institutions on the list of those to be informed of any compromised personally identifiable information when associated accounts are involved.

- **Disclosure of Breached Entity:** NAFCU believes that consumers should have the right to know which business entities have been breached. We urge Congress to mandate the disclosure of identities of companies and merchants whose data systems have been violated so consumers are aware of the ones that place their personal information at risk.

- **Enforcement of Prohibition on Data Retention:** NAFCU believes it is imperative to address the violation of existing agreements and law by merchants and retailers who retain payment card information electronically. Many entities do not respect this prohibition and store sensitive personal data in their systems, which can be breached easily in many cases.

- **Burden of Proof in Data Breach Cases:** In line with the responsibility for making consumers whole after they are harmed by a data breach, NAFCU believes that the evidentiary burden of proving a lack of fault should rest with the merchant or retailer who incurred the breach. These parties should have the duty to demonstrate that they took all necessary precautions to guard consumers' personal information but sustained a violation nonetheless. The law is currently vague on this issue, and NAFCU asks that this burden of proof be clarified in statute.

Again, on behalf of our nation's credit unions we thank you for your leadership on this issue and welcome the opportunity to work with you on legislation to strengthen data security standards for those who do not have such requirements now. If my staff or I can be of assistance to you, or if you have any questions regarding this issue, please feel free to contact myself, or NAFCU's Vice President of Legislative Affairs, Brad Thaler, at (703) 842-2204.

Sincerely,

B. Dan Berger
President and CEO

cc: Members of the Subcommittee on Financial Institutions and Consumer Credit

STATEMENT OF THE NATIONAL RETAIL FEDERATION FOR THE HOUSE FINANCIAL SERVICES SUBCOMMITTEE ON FINANCIAL INSTITUTIONS AND CONSUMER CREDIT

HEARING ON

"DATA SECURITY: EXAMINING EFFORTS TO PROTECT AMERICANS' FINANCIAL INFORMATION"

MARCH 5, 2014

National Retail Federation
325 7th Street, N.W., Suite 1100
Washington, D.C. 20004
(202) 783 –7971
www.nrf.com

Chairman Capito, Ranking Member Meeks, members of the Subcommittee, on behalf of the National Retail Federation (NRF) we want to thank you for giving us this opportunity to provide you with these comments on data security and protecting American's financial information. NRF is the world's largest retail trade association, representing discount and department stores, home goods and specialty stores, Main Street merchants, grocers, wholesalers, chain restaurants and Internet retailers from the United States and more than 45 countries. Retail is the nation's largest private sector employer, supporting one in four U.S. jobs – 42 million working Americans. Contributing $2.5 trillion to annual GDP, retail is a daily barometer for the nation's economy.

Collectively, retailers spend billions of dollars safeguarding consumers' data and fighting fraud. Data security is something that our members strive to improve every day. Virtually all of the data breaches we've seen in the United States during the past couple of months – from those at retailers that have been prominent in the news to those at banks and card network companies that have received less attention – have been perpetrated by criminals that are breaking the law. All of these companies are victims of these crimes and we should keep that in mind as we explore this topic and public policy initiatives relating to it.

This issue is one that we urge the Committee to examine in a holistic fashion: we need to reduce fraud. That is, we should not be satisfied with deciding what to do after a data breach occurs – who to notify and how to assign liability. Instead, it's important to look at why such breaches occur and what the perpetrators get out of them so that we can find ways to reduce and prevent not only the breaches themselves, but the fraudulent activity that is often the goal of these events. If breaches become less profitable to criminals then they will dedicate fewer resources to committing them and our goals will become more achievable.

With that in mind, these comments are designed to provide some background on data breaches and on fraud, explain how these events interact with our payments system, discuss some of the technological advancements that could improve the current situation, raise some ways to achieve those improvements, and then discuss the aftermath of data breaches and some ways to approach things when problems do occur.

Data Breaches in the United States

Unfortunately, data breaches are a fact of life in the United States. In its 2013 data breach investigations report, Verizon analyzed more than 47,000 security incidents and 621 confirmed data breaches that took place during the prior year. Virtually every part of the economy was hit in some way: 37% of breaches happened at financial institutions; 24% happened at retail; 20% happened at manufacturing, transportation and utility companies; and 20% happened at information and professional services firms.

It may be surprising to some given recent media coverage that more data breaches occur at financial institutions than at retailers. And, it should be noted, even these figures obscure the fact that there are far more merchants that are potential targets of criminals in this area. There are hundreds of times as many merchants accepting card payments in the United States than there are financial institutions issuing and processing those payments. So, proportionally, and not surprisingly, the thieves focus far more often on banks which have our most sensitive financial information – including not just card account numbers but bank account numbers, social security numbers and other identifying data that can be used to steal identities beyond completing some fraudulent transactions.

Who are the victims?

37% of breaches affected financial organizations (+)

24% of breaches occurred in retail environments and restaurants (-)

20% of network intrusions involved manufacturing, transportation, and utilities (+)

20% of network intrusions hit information and professional services firms (-)

38% of breaches impacted larger organizations (+)

27 different countries are represented

Victims in this report span restaurants, retailers, media companies, banks, utilities, engineering firms, multi-national corporations, security providers, defense contractors, government agencies, and more across the globe. A definite relationship exists between industry and attack motive, which is most likely a byproduct of the data targeted (e.g., stealing payment cards from retailers and intellectual property [IP] from manufacturers).

The ratio among organizational sizes is fairly even this time around, rather than tipping toward the small end of the scale as it did in our last report.

Source: 2013 Data Breach Investigations Report, Verizon

Nearly one-fifth of all of these breaches were perpetrated by state-affiliated actors connected to China. Three in four breaches were driven by financial motives. Two-thirds of the breaches took months or more to discover and 69% of all breaches were discovered by someone outside the affected organization.[1]

These figures are sobering. There are far too many breaches. And, breaches are often difficult to detect and carried out in many cases by criminals with real resources behind them. Financially focused crime seems to most often come from organized groups in Eastern Europe rather than state-affiliated actors in China, but the resources are there in both cases. The pressure on our financial system due to the overriding goal of many criminals intent on financial fraud is acute. We need to recognize that this is a continuous battle against determined fraudsters and be guided by that reality.

Background on Fraud

Fraud numbers raise similar concerns. Just a year ago, Forbes found that Mexico and the United States were at the top of the charts worldwide in credit and debit card fraud.[2] And fraud losses in the United States have been going up in recent years while some other countries have

[1] 2013 Data Breach Investigations Report, Verizon.

[2] "Countries with the most card fraud: U.S. and Mexico," *Forbes* by Halah Touryalai, Oct. 22, 2012.

had success reducing their fraud rates. The United States in 2012 accounted for nearly 30 percent of credit and debit card charges but 47 percent of all fraud losses.[3] Credit and debit card fraud losses totaled $11.27 billion in 2012.[4] And retailers spend $6.47 billion trying to prevent card fraud each year.[5]

Fraud is particularly devastating for retailers in the United States. LexisNexis and Javelin Strategy & Research have published an annual report on the "True Cost of Fraud" each year for the last several years. The 2009 report found, for example, that retailers suffer fraud losses that are 10 times higher than financial institutions and 20 times the cost incurred by consumers. This study covered more than just card fraud and looked at fraudulent refunds/returns, bounced checks, and stolen merchandise as well. Of the total, however, more than half of what merchants lost came from unauthorized transactions and card chargebacks.[6] The founder and President of Javelin Strategy, James Van Dyke, said at the time, "We weren't completely surprised that merchants are paying more than half of the share of the cost of unauthorized transactions as compared to financial institutions. But we were very surprised that it was 90-10."[7] Similarly, Consumer Reports wrote in June 2011, "The Mercator report estimates U.S. card issuers' total losses from credit- and debit-card fraud at $2.4 billion. That figure does not include losses that are borne by merchants, which probably run into tens of billions of dollars a year."[8]

Online fraud is a significant problem. It has jumped 36 percent from 2012 to 2013.[9] In fact, estimates are that online and other fraud in which there is no physical card present accounts for 90 percent of all card fraud in the United States.[10] And, not surprisingly, fraud correlates closely with data breaches among consumers. More than 22 percent of breach victims suffered fraud while less than 3 percent of consumers who didn't have their data breached experienced fraud.[11]

[3] "U.S. credit cards, chipless and magnetized, lure global fraudsters," by Howard Schneider, Hayley Tsukayama and Amrita Jayakumar, *Washington Post*, January 21, 2014.
[4] "Credit Card and Debit Card Fraud Statistics," CardHub 2013, available at http://www.cardhub.com/edu/credit-debit-card-fraud-statistics/.
[5] *Id.*
[6] A fraud chargeback is when the card-issuing bank and card network take the money for a transaction away from the retailer so that the retailer pays for the fraud.
[7] "Retailers are bearing the brunt: New report suggests what they can do to fight back," by M.V. Greene, NRF Stores, Jan. 2010.
[8] "House of Cards: Why your accounts are vulnerable to thieves," Consumer Reports, June 2011.
[9] 2013 True Cost of Fraud, LexisNexis at 6.
[10] "What you should know about the Target case," by Penny Crosman, *American Banker*, Jan. 23, 2014.
[11] 2013 True Cost of Fraud, LexisNexis at 20.

Figure 11. Fraud Incidence Rate Among All Consumers, Data Breach Victims, And Non Data Breach Victims (2010 -2012)

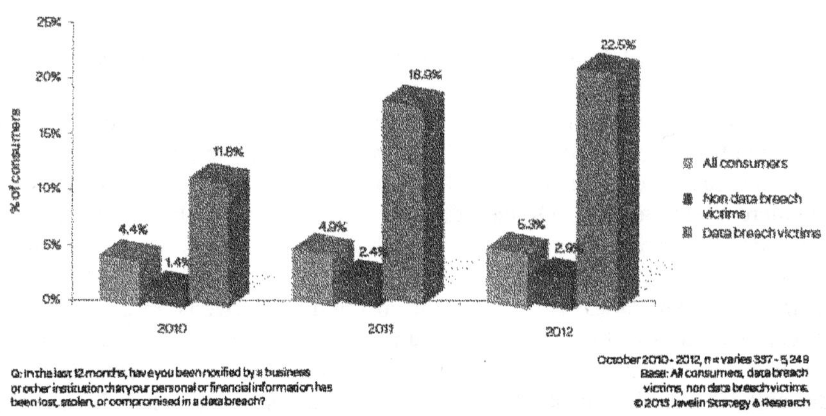

Source: 2013 True Cost of Fraud, LexisNexis

These numbers provide insights as to how to get to the right solutions of better safeguarding consumer and cardholder data and the need to improve authentication of transactions to protect against fraud. But before delving into those areas, some background on our payments system could be helpful.

The Payments System

Payments data is sought in breaches more often than any other type of data.[12] Now, every party in the payment system, financial institutions, networks, processors, retailers and consumers, has a role to play in reducing fraud. However, although all parties have a responsibility, some of those parties are integral to the system's design and promulgation while others, such as retailers and consumers, must work with the system as it is delivered to them.

As the following chart shows, while the banks are intimately connected to Visa and MasterCard, merchants and consumers have virtually no role in designing the payment system. Rather, they are bound to it by separate agreements issued by financial intermediaries.

[12] 2013 Data Breach Investigations Report, Verizon at 445, figure 35.

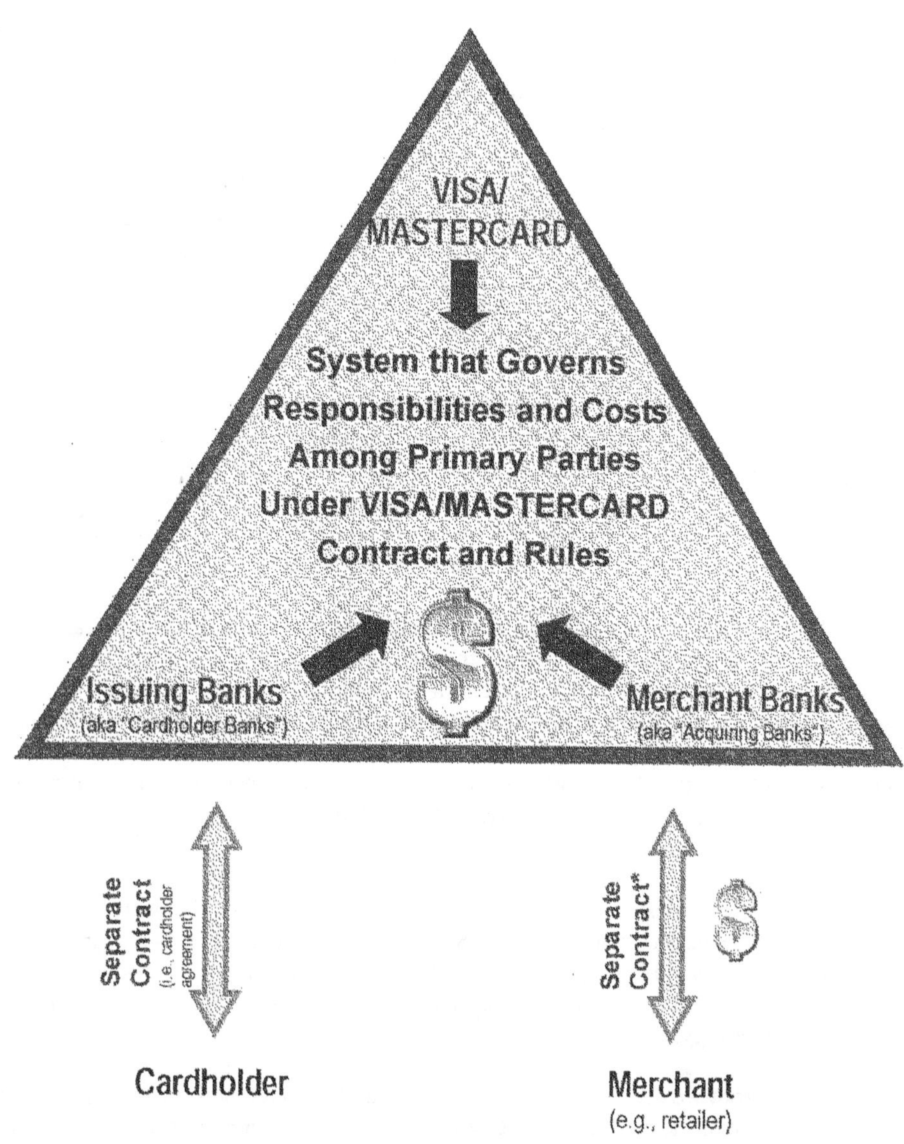

* Typically contract between merchant bank and its retailers requires retailers to reimburse merchant bank for any costs, penalties, or fees imposed by the system on the merchant bank (including chargebacks – i.e., disputed charges – and costs of data breaches)

Thus consumers are obligated to keep their cards safe and secure in their wallets and avoid misuse, but must necessarily turn their card data over to others in order to effectuate a transaction. Retailers are likewise obligated to collect and protect the card data they receive, but are obligated to deliver it to processors in order to complete a transaction, resolve a dispute or process a refund. In contrast, those inside the triangle have much more systemic control.

For example, retailers are essentially at the mercy of the dominant credit card companies when it comes to protecting payment card data. The credit card networks – Visa, MasterCard, American Express, Discover and JCB – are responsible for an organization known as the PCI (which stands for Payment Card Industry) data security council. PCI establishes data security standards (PCI-DSS) for payment cards. While well intentioned in concept, these standards have not worked quite as well in practice. They have been inconsistently applied, and their avowed purpose has been significantly altered.

PCI has in critical respects over time pushed card security costs onto merchants even when other decisions might have more effectively reduced fraud – or done so at lower cost. For example, retailers have long been required by PCI to encrypt the payment card information that they have. While that is appropriate, PCI has not required financial institutions to be able to accept that data in encrypted form. That means the data often has to be de-encrypted at some point in the process in order for transactions to be processed.

Similarly, merchants are expected to annually demonstrate PCI compliance to the card networks, often at considerable expense, in order to benefit from a promise that the merchants would be relieved of certain fraud inherent in the payment system, which PCI is supposed to prevent. However, certification by the networks as PCI Compliant apparently has not been able to adequately contain the growing fraud and retailers report that the "promise" increasingly has been abrogated or ignored. Unfortunately, as card security expert Avivah Litan of Gartner Research wrote recently, "The PCI (Payment Card Industry) security standard has largely been a failure when you consider its initial purpose and history."[13]

PCI has not addressed many obvious deficiencies in cards themselves. There has been much attention to the fact that the United States is one of the last places on earth to put card information onto magnetic stripes on the backs of cards that can easily be read and can easily be counterfeited (in part because that data is static and unchanging). We need to move past magstripe technology.

But, before we even get to that question, we need to recognize that sensitive card data is right on the front of the card, embossed with prominent characters. Simply seeing the front of a card is enough for some fraudsters and there have been fraud schemes devised to trick consumers into merely showing someone their cards. While having the embossed card number on the front of the card might have made sense in the days of knuckle-buster machines and carbon copies, those days are long passed.

In fact, cards include the cardholder's name, card number, expiration date, signature and card verification value (CVV) code. Everything a fraudster needs is right there on the card. The

[13] "How PCI Failed Target and U.S. Consumers," by Avivah Litan, Gartner Blog Network, Jan. 20, 2014, available at http://blogs.gartner.com/avivah-litan/2014/01/20/how-pci-failed-target-and-u-s-consumers/.

bottom line is that cards are poorly designed and fraud-prone products that the system has allowed to continue to proliferate.

PCI has also failed to require that the identity of the cardholder is actually verified or authenticated at the time of the transaction. Signatures don't do this. Not only is it easy to fake a signature, but merchants are not allowed by the major card networks to reject a transaction based on a deficient signature. So, the card networks clearly know a signature is a useless gesture which proves nothing more than that someone was there purporting to be the cardholder.

The use of personal identification numbers (PINs) has actually proven to be an effective way to authenticate the identity of the cardholder. PIN numbers are personal to each cardholder and do not appear on the cards themselves. While they are certainly not perfect, their use is effective at reducing fraud. On debit transactions, for example, PIN transactions have one-sixth the amount of fraud losses that signature transactions have.[14] But PINs are not required on credit card transactions. Why? From a fraud prevention perspective, there is no good answer except that the card networks which set the issuance standards have failed to protect people in a very basic way.

As noted by LexisNexis, merchant fraud costs are much higher than banks' fraud costs. When credit or debit card fraud occurs, Visa and MasterCard have pages of rules providing ways that banks may be able to charge back the transaction to the retailer (which is commonly referred to as a "chargeback"). That is, the bank will not pay the retailer the money for the fraudulent transaction even though the retailer provided the consumer with the goods in question. When this happens, and it happens a lot, the merchant loses the goods *and* the money on the sale. According to the Federal Reserve, this occurs more than 40 percent of the time when there is fraud on a signature debit transaction,[15] and our members tell us that the percentage is even higher on credit transactions. In fact, for online transactions, which as noted account for 90 percent of fraud, merchants pay for the vast majority of fraudulent transactions.[16]

Retailers have spent billions of dollars on card security measures and upgrades to comply with PCI card security requirements, but it hasn't made them immune to data breaches and fraud. The card networks have made those decisions for merchants and the increases in fraud demonstrate that their decisions have not been as effective as they should have been.

Improved Technology Solutions

There are technologies available that could reduce fraud. An overhaul of the fraud-prone cards that are currently used in the U.S. market is long overdue. As I noted, requiring the use of a PIN is one way to reduce fraud. Doing so takes a vulnerable piece of data (the card number) and makes it so that it cannot be used on its own. This ought to happen not only in the brick-

---

[14] *See* 77 Fed. Reg. 46261 (Aug. 3, 2012) reporting $1.11 billion in signature debit fraud losses and $181 million in PIN debit fraud losses.

[15] *Id.* at 46262.

[16] Merchants assume 74 percent of fraud losses for online and other card-not-present signature debit transactions. 77 Fed. Reg. 46262.

and-mortar environment in which a physical card is used but also in the online environment in which the physical card does not have to be used. Canada, for example, is exploring the use of a PIN for online purchases. The same should be true here. Doing so would help directly with the 90 percent of U.S. fraud which occurs online. It is not happenstance that automated teller machines (ATMs) require the entry of a PIN before dispensing cash. Using the same payment cards for purchases should be just as secure as using them at ATMs.

Cards should also be smarter and use dynamic data rather than magnetic stripes. In much of the world this is done using computer chips that are integrated into physical credit and debit cards. That is a good next step for the United States. It is important to note, however, that there are many types of technologies that may be employed to make this upgrade. EMV, which is an acronym for Europay, MasterCard and Visa, is merely one particular proprietary technology. As the name indicates, EMV was established by Europay, MasterCard and Visa. A proprietary standard could be a detriment to the other potentially competitive networks.[17] Adopting a closed system, such as EMV, means we are locking out the synergistic benefits of competition.

But even within that closed framework, it should also be noted that everywhere in the world that EMV has been deployed to date the card networks have required that the cards be used with a PIN. That makes sense. But here, the dominant card networks are proposing to force chips (or even EMV) on the U.S. market without requiring PIN authentication. Doing that makes no sense and loses a significant part of the fraud prevention benefits of chip technology. To do otherwise would mean that merchants would spend billions to install new card readers without they or their customers obtaining PINs' fraud-reducing benefits. We would essentially be spending billions to combine a 1990's technology (chips) with a 1960's relic (signature) in the face of 21st century threats.

Another technological solution that could help deter and prevent data breaches and fraud is encryption. Merchants are already required by PCI standards to encrypt cardholder data but, as noted earlier, not everyone in the payments chain is required to be able to accept data in encrypted form. That means that data may need to be de-encrypted at some points in the process. Experts have called for a change to require "end-to-end" (or point-to-point) encryption which is simply a way to describe requiring everyone in the payment-handling chain to accept, hold and transmit the data in encrypted form.

---

[17] There are issues with EMV because the technology is just one privately owned solution. For example, EMV includes specifications for near field communications that would form the technological basis of Visa and MasterCard's mobile payments solutions. That raises serious antitrust concerns for retailers because we are just starting to get some competitors exploring mobile payments. If the currently dominant card networks are able to lock-in their proprietary technology in a way that locks-out competition in mobile payments, that would be a bad result for merchants and consumers who might be on the verge of enjoying the benefits of some new innovations and competition.

So, while chip cards would be a step forward in terms of improving card products, if EMV is forced as the chip card technology that must be used – rather than an open-source chip technology which would facilitate competition and not predetermine mobile payment market-share – it could be a classic case of one step forward and two steps backward.

According to the September 2009 issue of the Nilson Report "most recent cyberattacks have involved intercepting data in transit from the point of sale to the merchant or acquirer's host, or from that host to the payments network." The reason this often occurs is that "data must be decrypted before being forwarded to a processor or acquirer because Visa, MasterCard, American Express, and Discover networks can't accept encrypted data at this time."[18]

Keeping sensitive data encrypted throughout the payments chain would go a long way to convincing fraudsters that the data is not worth stealing in the first place – at least, not unless they were prepared to go through the arduous task of trying to de-encrypt the data which would be necessary in order to make use of it. Likewise, using PIN-authentication of cardholders now would offer some additional protection against fraud should this decrypted payment data be intercepted by a criminal during its transmission "in the clear."

Tokenization is another variant that could be helpful. Tokenization is a system in which sensitive payment card information (such as the account number) is replaced with another piece of data (the "token"). Sensitive payment data could be replaced with a token to represent each specific transaction. Then, if a data breach occurred and the token data were stolen, it could not be used in any other transactions because it was unique to the transaction in question. This technology has been available in the payment card space since at least 2005.[19] Still, tokenization is not a panacea, and it is important that whichever form is adopted be an open standard so that a small number of networks not obtain a competitive advantage, by design, over other payment platforms

In many models tokenization occurs "after the fact" – generally post authorization. Thus some fraud risk remains. To deal with this point-to- point encryption is preferred and would be complimentary to tokenization. The former would occur between the card being read and the assignment of a token. From the merchant's perspective, tokenization involves significant operational changes and could carry significant out-of-pocket costs. Despite that, for the majority of transactions, tokenization still may not address both ends of the security/authentication equation as well as would PIN and Chip. It has greatest utility in the 6 percent of transactions that currently do not occur face-to-face. Consequently, while point-to-point encryption and tokenization could be valuable adjuncts to PIN and Chip authentication, they are not a substitute.

In addition, in some configurations, mobile payments offer the promise of greater security as well. In the mobile setting, consumers won't need to have a physical card – and they certainly won't replicate the security problem of physical cards by embossing their account numbers on the outside of their mobile phones. It should be easy for consumers to enter a PIN or password to use payment technology with their smart phones. Consumers are already used to accessing their phones and a variety of services on them through passwords. Indeed, if we are looking to leapfrog the already aging current technologies, mobile-driven payments may be the answer.

---

[18] The Nilson Report, Issue 934, Sept. 2009 at 7.

[19] For information on Shift4's 2005 launch of tokenization in the payment card space see http://www.internetretailer.com/2005/10/13/shift4-launches-security-tool-that-lets-merchants-re-use-credit.

Indeed, as much improved as they are, chips are essentially dumb computers. Their dynamism makes them significantly more advanced than magstripes, but their sophistication pales in comparison with the common smartphone. Smartphones contain computing powers that could easily enable comparatively state-of-the-art fraud protection technologies. The phones soon may be nearly ubiquitous, and if their payment platforms are open and competitive, they will only get better.

The dominant card networks have not made all of the technological improvements suggested above to make the cards issued in the United States more resistant to fraud, despite the availability of the technology and their adoption of it in many other developed countries of the world, including Canada, the United Kingdom, and most countries of Western Europe.

In this section, we have merely described some of the solutions available, but the United States isn't using any of them the way that it should be. While everyone in the payments space has a responsibility to do what they can to protect against fraud and data theft, the card networks have arranged the establishment of the data security requirements and yet, in light of the threats, there is much left to be desired.

A Better System

How can we make progress toward the types of solutions that would reduce the crimes of data theft and fraud? One thing seems clear at this point: we won't get there by doing more of the same. We need PIN-authentication of card holders, regardless of the chip technology used on newly issued cards. We also need chip cards that use open standards and allow for competition among payment networks as we move into a world of growing mobile commerce. Finally, we need companies throughout the payment system to work together on achieving end-to-end encryption so that there are no weak links in the system where sensitive card payment information may be acquired more easily than in other parts of the system.

Steps Taken by Retailers After Discovery of a Breach of Security

In our view, it is after a fulsome evaluation of data breaches, fraud, the payments system and how to improve each of those areas in order to deter and prevent problems that we should turn to the issue of what to do when breaches occur. Casting blame and trying to assign liability is, at best, putting the cart before the horse and, at worst, an excuse for some actors to ignore their own responsibility for trying to prevent these crimes.

One cannot reasonably demand greater security of a system than the system is reasonably capable of providing. Some participants act as if the system is more robust than it is. Currently, when the existing card products are hit in a criminal breach, that company is threatened from many sides. The threats come from entities seeking to exact fines and taking other penalizing action even before the victimized company can secure its network from further breaches and determine through a forensic analysis what has happened in order to notify potentially affected customers. For example, retailers that have suffered a breach are threatened with fines for the breach based on allegations of non-compliance with PCI rules (even when the company has been certified as PCI-compliant). Other actors may expect the breached party to pay for all of the fraudulent transactions that take place on card accounts that were misused, even though the design of the cards facilitated their subsequent counterfeiting. Indeed, some have seriously suggested that retailers reimburse financial institutions for the cost of reissuing more fraud-prone cards. And, as a consequence of the breach, some retailers must then pay higher fees on its card transactions going forward. Retailers pay for these breaches over and over again, despite often times being victims of sophisticated criminal methods not reasonably anticipated prior to the attack.

Breaches require retailers to devote significant resources to remedy the breach, help inform customers and take preventative steps to ward off future attacks and any other potential vulnerabilities discovered in the course of the breach investigation. Weeks or months of forensic analysis may be necessary to definitively discover the cause and scope of the breach. Any discovered weaknesses must be shored up. Quiet and cooperative law enforcement efforts may be necessary in an effort to identify and capture the criminals. Indeed, law enforcement may temporarily discourage publication of the breach so as to not alert the perpetrators that their efforts have been detected.

It is worth noting that in some of these cases involving payment card data, retailers discover that they actually were not the source of the breach and that someone else in the payments chain was victimized or the network intrusion and theft occurred during the transmission of the payment card data between various participants in the system. For this reason, early attempts to assign blame and shift costs are often misguided and policy makers should take heed of the fact that often the earliest reports are the least accurate. Additionally, policy makers should consider that there is no independent organization devoted to determining where a breach occurred, and who is to blame – these questions are often raised in litigation that can last for years. This is another reason why it is best to at least wait until the forensic analysis has been completed to determine what happened. Even then, there may be questions unanswered if the attack and technology used was sophisticated enough to cover the criminals' digital tracks.

The reality is that when a criminal breach occurs, particularly in the payments system, all of the businesses that participate in that system and their shared customers are victimized. Rather than resort to blame and shame, parties should work together to ensure that the breach is remedied and steps are taken to prevent future breaches of the same type and kind.

Legislative Solutions

In addition to the marketplace and technological solutions suggested above, NRF also supports a range of legislative solutions that we believe would help improve the security of our networked systems, ensure better law enforcement tools to address criminal intrusions, and standardize and streamline the notification process so that consumers may be treated equally across the nation when it comes to notification of data security breaches.

From many consumers' perspective payment cards are payment cards. As has been often noted, consumers would be surprised to learn that their legal rights, when using a debit card – i.e. their own money – are significantly less than when using other forms of payment, such as a credit card. It would be appropriate if policy makers took steps to ensure that consumers' reasonable expectations were fulfilled, and they received at least the same level of legal protection when using their debit cards as they do when paying with credit.

In addition, NRF supports the passage by Congress of the bipartisan "Cyber Intelligence Sharing and Protection Act" (H.R. 624) so that the commercial sector can lawfully share information about cyber-threats in real-time and enable companies to defend their own networks as quickly as possible from cyber-attacks as soon as they are detected elsewhere by other business.

We also support legislation that provides more tools to law enforcement to ensure that unauthorized network intrusions and other criminal data security breaches are thoroughly investigated and prosecuted, and that the criminals that breach our systems to commit fraud with our customers' information are swiftly brought to justice.

Finally, and for nearly a decade, NRF has supported passage of legislation that would establish one, uniform federal breach notification law that would be modeled on, and preempt, the varying breach notification laws currently in operation in 46 states, the District of Columbia and federal territories. A federal law could ensure that all entities handling the same type of sensitive consumer information, such as payment card data, are subject to the same statutory rules and penalties with respect to notifying consumers of a breach affecting that information, Further, a preemptive federal breach notification law would allow retailers and other businesses that have been victimized by a criminal breach to focus their resources on remedying the breach and notifying consumers rather than hiring outside legal assistance to help guide them through the myriad and sometimes conflicting set of 50 data breach notification standards in the state and federal jurisdictions. Additionally, the use of one set of standardized notice rules would permit the offering to consumers of the same notice and the same rights regardless of where they live.

Conclusion

In closing three points are uppermost.

First, retailers take the increasing incidence of payment card fraud very seriously. We do so as Main Street members of the community, because it affects our neighbors and our customers. We do so as businesses, because it affects the bottom line. Merchants already bear at least an equal, and often a greater, cost of fraud than any other participant in the payment card system. We have every reason to want to see fraud reduced, but we have only a portion of the ability to make that happen. We did not design the system; we do not configure the cards; we do not issue the cards. We will work to effectively upgrade the system, but we cannot do it alone.

Second, the vast majority of breaches are criminal activity. The hacked party, whether a financial institution, a card network, a processor, a merchant, a governmental institution, or a consumer is the victim of a crime. Traditionally, we don't blame the victim of violence for the resulting stains; we should be similarly cautious about penalizing the hackee for the hack. The payment system is complicated. Every party has a role to play; we need to play it together. No system is invulnerable to the most sophisticated and dedicated of thieves. Consequently, eliminating all fraud is likely to remain an aspiration. Nevertheless, we will do our part to help achieve that goal.

Third, it is long past time for the U.S. to adopt PIN and chip card technology. The PIN authenticates and protects the consumer and the merchant. The chip authenticates the card to the bank. If the goal is to reduce fraud we must, at a minimum, do both.

Respectfully submitted,

Mallory B. Duncan
Senior Vice President, General Counsel
National Retail Federation

JEB HENSARLING, TX, CHAIRMAN

United States House of Representatives
Committee on Financial Services
Washington, D.C. 20515

MAXINE WATERS, CA, RANKING MEMBER

January 10, 2014

The Honorable Jeb Hensarling
Chairman
Committee on Financial Services
U.S. House of Representatives
Washington, D.C. 20515

Dear Chairman Hensarling:

The Target Corporation recently acknowledged that from November 27 to December 15, 2013, hackers stole credit and debit card information including card numbers, expirations dates and security codes for 40 million accounts, and other personally identifiable information for as many as 70 million customers. Accordingly, we respectfully request that you convene a full Financial Services Committee hearing to review the recent data breach including the adequacy of current consumer financial data security protection laws, and what Congress and industry stakeholders can proactively do to ensure the future security of consumers' card information.

We note that the Committee's oversight plan for the 113th Congress states that "building on the Committee's long-standing role in developing laws governing the handling of sensitive personal financial information about consumers including the Gramm-Leach-Bliley Act and the Fair and Accurate Credit Transactions Act (FACT Act), the Committee will continue to evaluate best practices for protecting the security and confidentiality of such information from any loss, unauthorized access, or misuse."

The Target breach—which industry analysts say is among the largest recorded financial data security breaches—raises important questions about what merchants who suspect a data breach has occurred must disclose, when they must disclose it, and who has the right to be notified. Quick notification of a breach increases the likelihood that consumers can take measures to protect themselves from fraudulent activity and is similarly critical to successfully reducing the ultimate fraud losses that financial institutions incur.

It is incumbent upon our Committee to explore whether industry data protection standards are appropriate, and examine whether heightened regulatory standards are needed to more effectively protect consumers. A hearing would provide members the opportunity to hear from regulators and the industry to learn what steps merchants, financial institutions, payment processers, card networks and others should take to reduce vulnerabilities in the payment system, and strengthen measures that protect consumers from fraud.

Consumers deserve reasonable assurances that the use of their credit or debit card will not jeopardize their financial and other personally identifiable information. This is increasingly important as companies continue to amass vast amounts of consumers' sensitive personal information.

We appreciate your attention to this request.

Sincerely,

Question#:	1
Topic:	Large companies
Hearing:	Data Security: Examining Efforts to Protect Americans' Financial Information
Primary:	The Honorable Kyrsten Sinema
Committee:	FINANCIAL SERVICES (HOUSE)

Question: Large companies such as Honeywell, Charles Schwab, and American Express have security teams with significant resources and investors. However, smaller innovative business like Bishop Fox and Securosis excel in this high-tech space as well. What are we doing to support them in terms of access to high-skilled labor and capital? How are we ensuring that the standards and regulations we create help – not hurt – these small businesses?

Response: The government and the private sector have a shared interest in ensuring the security and resilience of critical infrastructure, and the provision of essential services, under all conditions. Critical infrastructure owners and operators are often the greatest beneficiary of investing in their own security, including risk-based adoption of best practices for cybersecurity.

Executive Order 13636, Improving Critical Infrastructure Cybersecurity, directed the National Institute for Standards and Technology (NIST) to work with stakeholders to develop a voluntary framework based on existing standards, guidelines, and practices for reducing cyber risks to critical infrastructure. The Framework, created through collaboration between industry and government, has a prioritized, flexible, repeatable, and cost-effective approach to help owners and operators of critical infrastructure to manage cybersecurity-related risk.

The Critical Infrastructure Cyber Community, or C^3 (pronounced "C Cubed"), Voluntary Program is the coordination point within the Federal government for critical infrastructure owners and operators interested in improving their cyber risk management processes. The C^3 Voluntary Program aims to: 1) support industry in increasing its cyber resilience; 2) increase awareness and use of the Framework; and 3) encourage organizations to manage cybersecurity as part of an all hazards approach to enterprise risk management of critical infrastructure.

In February, the Department of Homeland Security (DHS) issued a Request for Information (RFI) seeking information from industry on its capacity to provide broadly scalable cyber security solutions at an affordable cost to small and medium businesses in support of adoption of the NIST Framework. Small and medium businesses have a need for an appropriate level of cyber security capabilities as they face cyber security threats and challenges with limited resources, capacity, and/or personnel. With this RFI, DHS is seeking to understand the landscape of capabilities available to small and medium businesses, and to help those businesses find ways to exploit those capabilities in order to

Question#:	1
Topic:	Large companies
Hearing:	Data Security: Examining Efforts to Protect Americans' Financial Information
Primary:	The Honorable Kyrsten Sinema
Committee:	FINANCIAL SERVICES (HOUSE)

make effective use of rapid advances in cyber security and technology. As DHS prepares to assume leadership of the National Initiative for Cybersecurity Education (NICE), we look forward to Congress' support in developing innovative cyber training for the private and public sector cybersecurity jobs that are the underpinning of cybersecurity.

Our goals are convergent: small and medium businesses want to manage their cyber risk and focus operationally, while DHS seeks to better equip smaller companies to manage their cyber risks according to their level of vulnerability and impact. At the same time, we are encouraging larger industry partners to invest in raising the level of cybersecurity across the field so we are all able to benefit from the network effect of increased security and reliability.

Question#:	2
Topic:	cybersecurity industry
Hearing:	Data Security: Examining Efforts to Protect Americans' Financial Information
Primary:	The Honorable Kyrsten Sinema
Committee:	FINANCIAL SERVICES (HOUSE)

Question: As the world continues to technically evolve, the cybersecurity industry will be a job creator for years, perhaps decades, to come. These are high-earning jobs and we need to make sure they stay in the U.S. What are we doing to ensure that small cybersecurity firms like Bishop Fox and Securosis have the resources and tools they need to develop a strong cybersecurity industry that creates jobs and protects our economic and national security interests?

Response:

Cyber Workforce and Training

We share your concerns about creating and maintaining a dynamic, cutting-edge workforce and ensuring that they have the opportunities to work for American cybersecurity goals. Within DHS, the Office of the Chief Human Capital Officer (OCHCO) obtained a Schedule A hiring authority, in September of 2009, in order to staff certain cyber security positions within the Department. This was in response to the Comprehensive National Cybersecurity Initiative (CNCI) established in January 2008. The Office of Personnel Management (OPM) granted the authority to DHS for up to 1,000 cyber security positions for which unique qualifications are required, and that are not currently established by OPM. DHS Components may make permanent, time-limited and temporary appointments in several occupational series. Additionally, the National Protection and Programs Directorate (NPPD) utilizes the IT Specialist (INFOSEC) Government wide direct hire authority to fill cyber related positions. Codifying recruitment and retention authorities commensurate with the Department of Defense and the Intelligence Community would ensure that the Department can quickly hire and offer a salary comparable to its partner agencies.

The federal government has been working on cybersecurity awareness and training for the past five years under the National Initiative for Cyber Education (NICE). This is a national program that encompasses a broad range of cyber education-focused activities, both internally for the federal workforce, but also externally to promote skills development in the Nation's workforce.

Some examples of successful job-related training that the NICE has sponsored include:

- Centers for Academic Excellence
- Scholarship for Service
- Cyber Competitions including the National Collegiate Cyber Defense Competition

Question#:	2
Topic:	cybersecurity industry
Hearing:	Data Security: Examining Efforts to Protect Americans' Financial Information
Primary:	The Honorable Kyrsten Sinema
Committee:	FINANCIAL SERVICES (HOUSE)

We are now in the process of updating the strategic plan and priorities for the NICE program. This update will include transitioning coordination of the NICE program to DHS, and strengthening the participation of other federal partners including NIST, NSF, and DOD. The updated strategy will also prioritize the development and promotion of job-related training for cybersecurity, in partnership with the private sector and state and local governments.

Cybersecurity Resources for Small and Medium Businesses

To ensure that small and medium businesses have the resources and support that they need to operate profitably while managing their cyber risk responsibly, DHS specifically targets small and medium businesses for support in a number of partner outreach initiatives. The C^3 Voluntary Program is a unique public-private initiative that supports practical application of the Framework. It facilitates:

- Forums for knowledge sharing and collaboration related to Framework use with other program participants;
- Access to freely available technical assistance to strengthen capabilities to manage cyber risks—this includes the National Cybersecurity Workforce Framework, access to the NICCS portal which contains cybersecurity workforce development and management tools, and training to enhance workforce skills;
- Opportunities to influence peers and other partners in the critical infrastructure community; and
- Assistance with meeting fiduciary responsibilities to manage cyber risks consistently.

DHS also continues to participate in the Small Business Innovative Research (SBIR) program with the release of one or two topics per year that address the research, development and transition of cyber security tools, methodologies, and products.

Question#:	3
Topic:	industry standards
Hearing:	Data Security: Examining Efforts to Protect Americans' Financial Information
Primary:	The Honorable Kyrsten Sinema
Committee:	FINANCIAL SERVICES (HOUSE)

Question: Business, policymakers and law enforcement must work together to protect our economic interests and national security. As we work to improve industry standards, we must ensure that government and industry coordinate to the greatest degree possible. Can you elaborate on the current level of coordination between government and industry stakeholders? What can be done to improve coordination?

Response: Coordination and collaboration between industry and government is key to strong cybersecurity. DHS is constantly striving to improve coordination and has a number of programs and initiatives dedicated to forging and maintaining private sector relationships at every level. Those relationships include the partnerships with critical infrastructure owners and operators to ensure cohesive cybersecurity efforts; the C^3 Voluntary program offering cybersecurity resources to private and public sector entities through DHS; information sharing programs available through Enhanced Cybersecurity Services (ECS); as well as ongoing collaboration with the private sector through the National Cybersecurity and Communications Integration Center (NCCIC), DHS's 24/7 center for cybersecurity incident response, protection and mitigation.

The Cyber Information Sharing and Collaboration Program (CISCP), which began in January 2012, established a systematic approach to cyber threat information sharing and collaboration between critical infrastructure and key resources and across all critical infrastructure sectors. Partners who have signed the CISCP Cooperative Research and Development Agreement (CRADA) share unclassified, actionable, timely threat indicator data (**not** incident data). Collaboration meetings are held monthly at the unclassified level and quarterly at the classified secret level.

Program Snapshot:

- 74 CRADA signatories
- 8 critical infrastructure Information Sharing and Analysis Centers plus 66 individual commercial entities, covering all 16 critical infrastructure sectors
- 78 entities in CRADA negotiations
- Approximately 25,000 indicators shared to date
- Data sharing ratio is approximately 75 percent government to 25 percent industry (currently five federal government furnished indicator providers)

Question#:	3
Topic:	industry standards
Hearing:	Data Security: Examining Efforts to Protect Americans' Financial Information
Primary:	The Honorable Kyrsten Sinema
Committee:	FINANCIAL SERVICES (HOUSE)

Recent success stories include an article describing CISCP's work providing "bulletins provided in formats that computers can 'read' so they can apply the appropriate protections. And containment recommendations are pumped out in plain text that people can read." ("DHS Quietly Delivers Hacker Footprints to Industry," Aliya Sternstein for *Nextgov*, April 2, 2014).

Specifically with respect to cyber threat intelligence, DHS's Office of Intelligence & Analysis (I&A) conducts cyber threat intelligence outreach and engagements with key critical infrastructure sectors at the broadest level possible, with an emphasis on improving the quality of unclassified cyber threat intelligence. DHS's I&A provides tailored analysis of cyber threat activity to various private sector, State and local, and Federal partners to develop a common, baseline understanding of cyber threats and enable decision-makers to protect, prevent, and mitigate against cyber threats. From FY 2012 to FY 2013, in the spirit of Executive Order 13636 guidance to expand information sharing, I&A robustly increased written unclassified and classified cyber intelligence production by 147% – 49 products to 121 products – and direct unclassified cyber threat briefings by 382% – 17 events to 82 events. In addition to that aggressive focus on unclassified support to DHS customers, the total increase in both unclassified and classified briefings jumped from FY 2012 to FY 2013 by 447% – 38 events to 208 events – and has continued in FY 2014 with 169 direct cyber threat briefings already delivered, representing an increase by a further 93% in overall FY 2013 outreach, to date.

The Cybersecurity Framework that was developed by NIST in fulfillment of Executive Order 13636, helps our private sector partners better identify, assess, and manage their cyber risks. DHS is developing the C^3 Voluntary Program to assist critical infrastructure in their adoption of the Framework, and to extend a range of cybersecurity resources, including:

- Information on cyber threats and vulnerabilities;
- Cybersecurity incident resources including the NCCIC, the United States Computer Emergency Readiness Team, and the Industrial Control Systems Cyber Emergency Response Team;
- Software assurance programs; and
- Technical resources such as cybersecurity strategy development, cybersecurity assessment tools, cyber exercise planning, cybersecurity risk management training, cybersecurity resilience review, a national vulnerability database, and roadmaps to enhance cybersecurity in certain sectors.

Question#:	3
Topic:	industry standards
Hearing:	Data Security: Examining Efforts to Protect Americans' Financial Information
Primary:	The Honorable Kyrsten Sinema
Committee:	FINANCIAL SERVICES (HOUSE)

The ECS program is a voluntary information sharing program that assists critical infrastructure owners and operators to improve protection of their systems from unauthorized access, exploitation, or data exfiltration. ECS consists of the operational processes and security oversight required to share sensitive and classified cyber threat information with qualified Commercial Service Providers (CSP) that will enable them to better protect their customers who are critical infrastructure entities. The ECS program develops threat "indicators" with this information and provides CSPs with those indicators of active, malicious cybersecurity activity. CSPs may use these threat indicators to provide approved cybersecurity services to critical infrastructure entities.

In ongoing day to day operations, the NCCIC is responsible for coordinating the national protection, mitigation, and recovery from both cyber and communications incidents. The NCCIC works closely with all levels of government and with the private sector and international partners, and invites stakeholders in government and industry to send representatives to the NCCIC floor, where information collection, analysis and distribution occurs around the clock. Since 2009, the NCCIC has responded to nearly half a million incident reports and released more than 26,000 actionable cybersecurity alerts to the Department's public and private sector partners.

www.ingramcontent.com/pod-product-compliance
Lightning Source LLC
Chambersburg PA
CBHW080421060326
40689CB00019B/4324